Focus on Vocabulary Learning

Oxford Key Concepts for the Language Classroom series

Focus on Assessment
Eunice Eunhee Jang

Focus on Content-Based Language Teaching
Patsy M. Lightbown

Focus on Grammar and Meaning
Luciana C. de Oliveira and Mary J. Schleppegrell

Focus on Learning Technologies
Nicky Hockly

Focus on Literacy
Danling Fu and Marylou M. Matoush

Focus on Oral Interaction
Rhonda Oliver and Jenefer Philp

Focus on Reading
Esther Geva and Gloria Ramírez

Focus on Special Educational Needs
Cristina Sánchez-López and Theresa Young

Focus on Vocabulary Learning
Marlise Horst

Focus on Vocabulary Learning

Marlise Horst

UNIVERSITY PRESS

Great Clarendon Street, Oxford, OX2 6DP, United Kingdom

Oxford University Press is a department of the University of Oxford.
It furthers the University's objective of excellence in research, scholarship,
and education by publishing worldwide. Oxford is a registered trade
mark of Oxford University Press in the UK and in certain other countries

© Oxford University Press 2019

The moral rights of the author have been asserted

First published in 2019

2023 2022 2021 2020 2019
10 9 8 7 6 5 4 3 2 1

No unauthorized photocopying

All rights reserved. No part of this publication may be reproduced, stored
in a retrieval system, or transmitted, in any form or by any means, without
the prior permission in writing of Oxford University Press, or as expressly
permitted by law, by licence or under terms agreed with the appropriate
reprographics rights organization. Enquiries concerning reproduction
outside the scope of the above should be sent to the ELT Rights Department,
Oxford University Press, at the address above

You must not circulate this work in any other form and you must impose
this same condition on any acquirer

Links to third party websites are provided by Oxford in good faith and for
information only. Oxford disclaims any responsibility for the materials
contained in any third party website referenced in this work

ISBN: 978 0 19 400313 1

ACKNOWLEDGEMENTS

The author and publisher are grateful to those who have given permission to reproduce the following extracts and adaptations of copyright material: p.5 Extract from ALERT Corpus 2: Teacher talk in an adult ESL Classroom. Reproduced by permission. p.24 Extract from Kieffer, M. J., & Lesaux, N. K. (2007). 'Breaking down words to build meaning: Morphology, vocabulary, and reading comprehension in the urban classroom', *The Reading Teacher*, 61(2), pp.134–144. John Wiley and Sons. Reproduced by permission. p.25 Extract from Paribakht, T., & Wesche, M. (1996). 'Vocabulary enhancement activities and reading for meaning in second language vocabulary acquisition'. In J. Coady & T. Huckin (Eds.), *Second Language Vocabulary Acquisition: A Rationale for Pedagogy*, pp.174–200. Cambridge: Cambridge University Press. p.30 Extract from Hedgecock, J. S., & Ferris, D. R. (2018). *Teachers readers of English: Students, texts, and contexts*. CCC Republication. Reprinted by permission. p.45 Extract from Joe, A., Nation, p., & Newton, J. (1996). 'Vocabulary learning and speaking activities' by Angela Joe, Paul Nation, & Jonathan Newton, *English Teaching Forum*, 34(1), pp.2–7. Reproduced by permission. pp.57-58 Oxford Bookworms graded readers corpus © Oxford University Press. Used with permission. pp.76–77 Hart, B., & Risley, T. R. (1995). *Meaningful differences in the everyday experience of young American children*. Reprinted by permission of Brookes Publishing. pp.85–86 Participant interview from White, J., & Horst, M. (2006-2009). 'Bridging the gap between first and second languages at school'. Reproduced by permission. pp.88–90 Writing samples from Horst, M., & Collins, L. (2006). 'Faible to strong: How does their vocabulary grow?', *The Canadian Modern Language Review*, 63(1), pp.83–106. p.65 Extract from Scott, J., Skobell, B., & Wells, J. (2016). 'The word-conscious classroom: Building the vocabulary readers and writers need'. Reproduced by permission. pp.94, 97, 99 Extract from Baker, S., Lesaux, N., Jayanthi, M., Dimino, J., Proctor, C. p., Morris, J., Gersten, R., Haymond, K., Kieffer, M. J., Linan-Thompson, S., & Newman-Gonchar, R. (2014). *Teaching academic content and literacy to English learners in elementary and middle school (NCEE 2014–4012)*. Washington, DC: National Center for Education Evaluation and Regional Assistance (NCEE), Institute of Education Sciences, U.S. Department of Education. Retrieved from the NCEE website: http://ies.ed.gov/ncee/wwc/publications_reviews.aspx. pp.104–105 Extract from Nation, p., & Beglar, D. (2007). *Vocabulary Size Test (monolingual, 20,000, Version A)*. Reproduced by permission. p.115 Extract from Pacheco, M. B., & Goodwin, A. (2013). 'Putting two and two together: Middle school students' morphological problem-solving strategies for unknown words', *Journal of Adolescent & Adult Literacy*, 56(7), pp.541–553. John Wiley and Sons. Reproduced by permission. p.116 Extract from Lee, S. H., & Muncie, J. (2006). 'From receptive to productive: Improving ESL learners' use of vocabulary in a postreading composition task'. *TESOL Quarterly* 40(2), pp.295–320. p.122–123 Extract from Nation, P. (1990). *Teaching and learning vocabulary*. Heinle Thompson ELT. Reproduced by permission. pp.124–125 Extract from Haastrup, K. (1991). *Lexical inferencing procedures, or, talking about words: Receptive procedures in foreign language learning with special reference to English*. Tübingen: Gunter Narr Verlag. p.126 Extract from 'Structure' concordance lines from Brown Corpus, computational analysis of present-day American English. Kučera & Francis (1967) Concordance generated on May 22, 2018. Kučera & Francis (1967) Concordance generated on May 22, 2018.

Although every effort has been made to trace and contact copyright holders before publication, this has not been possible in some cases. We apologize for any apparent infringement of copyright and if notified, the publisher will be pleased to rectify any errors or omissions at the earliest opportunity.

To the learners and their teachers.

Contents

Acknowledgments	xi
Series Editors' Preface	xii
Introduction	1
1 Vocabulary Knowledge and Learning Goals	**5**
Preview	5
What is Vocabulary Learning?	8
Which Words are Important to Know?	10
Corpora and Frequent Words	10
Coverage	12
Deciding Which Words to Teach	15
High-Frequency Vocabulary	16
Mid-Frequency Vocabulary	17
Low-Frequency Vocabulary	17
Academic Vocabulary and Domain-Specific Words	18
Which Word List?	22
Dimensions of Vocabulary Development	24
Partial to Precise Knowledge	24
Depth of Knowledge	26
Receptive and Productive Knowledge	27
Components of Vocabulary Knowledge	29
Form	29
Meaning	32
Use	34
Summary	36
2 Learning Vocabulary	**37**
Preview	37
Setting the Scene	37
Theories of Vocabulary Acquisition	39
Behaviorist Perspectives	39
The Usage-Based Perspective	41

Information Processing	44
Noticing, Retrieval, Elaboration	48
Vocabulary Acquisition at School	54
Reading and the Vocabulary of School	55
Incidental Vocabulary Learning	58
Incidental Acquisition Through Reading	59
Comprehensibility and Volume	60
Supporting Word Learning Through Reading	62
Word Learning Through Viewing	63
The Sociocultural Perspective	64
Summary	66
3 Vocabulary Acquisition in Young Learners of English	**69**
Preview	69
English Vocabulary Growth in Primary School	69
How Much? How Fast?	71
Explanations for Growth	73
L2 Word Knowledge in Development	87
Productive Vocabulary in Use	88
Vocabulary Depth	90
Teaching the Vocabulary of School	91
Selecting Words	92
Teaching Academic Vocabulary	96
Summary	100
4 Vocabulary Acquisition in Adolescent Learners of English	**101**
Preview	101
Adolescent Learners of English	101
English Vocabulary Growth in Adolescents	103
How Much? How Fast?	103
Support for Vocabulary Learning at School	109
Explanations for Growth	110
L2 Word Knowledge in Development	113
Productive Use	115
Teaching the Vocabulary of School	118
Selecting Words	118
Teaching Academic Vocabulary	119

Inferencing Skills	121
Concordancing	125
Word Cards	128
Summary	129
5 Vocabulary: What We Know Now	131
Preview	131
Reflecting on Ideas about Learning Second Language Vocabulary: Learning from Research	131
Conclusion	139
Suggestions for Further Reading	141
Appendix	145
Glossary	149
References	159
Index	171

Acknowledgments

The story of this book begins with a fortuitous meeting in the spring of 1993, when Patsy Lightbown, now co-editor of the Key Concepts series and then my university professor, introduced me to Paul Meara, who eventually became my PhD supervisor. Through him, I came to know a vibrant and supportive international community of vocabulary researchers. I have learned more than I can say from their work, and their friendship has been a source of inspiration for many years. I am also grateful for the new insights working on this book has brought. I was taken out of the familiar zone of university education and into the world of young learners and adolescents. Discovering the work of educators and researchers so deeply committed to improving the lives and learning opportunities of their students has opened my eyes. I am full of admiration for the difficult work they do. Many names appear in this book, but I was not able to include all of the valuable publications I have learned from. I hope I have acknowledged those whose work I have drawn on directly. I cannot emphasize enough how much I have benefitted from the insights of teachers and students over a lifetime of work in the Middle East, Asia, and Canada. It was through teaching learners of English that I came to see how important it is to know vocabulary.

I thank series editors Patsy Lightbown and Nina Spada for giving me the opportunity to write this book. Your confidence gave me confidence. So many helpful, graciously worded suggestions! Special thanks to Tim Herdon, Sarah Finch, and Sophie Rogers of Oxford University Press for their support and close attention to detail. Thanks also to friends and colleagues at Concordia University for their thoughtful advice and concrete answers to questions. Finally, I will never forget working on vocabulary lists with Tom Cobb in Riyadh in the 1980s, when computers were primitive and making a textbook corpus meant typing out whole books manually. Thanks, Tom, for thinking about vocabulary with me—then and now.

Series Editors' Preface

The Oxford Key Concepts for the Language Classroom series is designed to provide accessible information about research on topics that are important to second language teachers. Each volume focuses on a particular area of second/foreign language learning and teaching, covering both background research and classroom-based studies. The emphasis is on how knowing about this research can guide teachers in their instructional planning, pedagogical activities, and assessment of learners' progress.

The idea for the series was inspired by the book *How Languages are Learned*. Many colleagues have told us that they appreciate the way that book can be used either as part of a university teacher education program or in a professional development course for experienced teachers. They have commented on the value of publications that show teachers and future teachers how knowing about research on language learning and teaching can help them think about their own teaching principles and practices.

This series is oriented to the educational needs and abilities of school-aged children (5–18 years old), with distinct chapters focusing on research that is specific to primary- and secondary-level learners. The volumes are written for second language teachers, whether their students are minority language speakers learning the majority language or students learning a foreign language in a classroom far from the communities where the language is spoken. Some of the volumes will be useful to 'mainstream' teachers who have second language learners among their students, but have limited training in second/foreign language teaching. Some of the volumes will also be primarily for teachers of English, whereas others will be of interest to teachers of other languages as well.

The series includes volumes on topics that are key for second language teachers of school-age children, and each volume is written by authors whose research and teaching experience have focused on learners and teachers in this age group. While much has been written about some of these topics, most publications are either 'how to' methodology texts with no explicit link to research, or academic works that are designed for researchers and postgraduate students who require a thorough scholarly treatment of the research, rather than an overview and interpretation for classroom practice. Instructors in programs for teachers often find that the methodology texts lack the academic background appropriate for a university course and that the scholarly works are too long, too difficult, or not sufficiently classroom-oriented for the needs of teachers and future teachers. The volumes in this series are intended to bridge that gap.

The books are enriched by the inclusion of *Spotlight Studies* that represent important research and *Classroom Snapshots* that provide concrete examples of teaching/learning events in the second language classroom. In addition, through a variety of activities, readers will be able to integrate this information with their own experiences of learning and teaching.

Introduction

In schools around the world, learners face the challenge of studying academic subjects in a language that is not the one they learned at home. For many of these learners, the new language of school is English. Young learners of English—Spanish-speaking immigrant learners in North American schools, for example—can often master basic spoken English used in conversations on the playground or in the street rather quickly. While this is a substantial accomplishment, it is not enough. Studying in English requires mastery of a new kind of language that uses a special vocabulary. The words of school are formal and often abstract (*aspect*, *process*, and *equip*, for example); they are more likely to be found in writing than in speech. Learners of English need to know thousands of these 'school' words and to be able to use them effectively in reading textbooks, understanding explanations, presenting reports, taking tests, and more. In recent years, educators, researchers and policymakers have come to see knowledge of vocabulary as the key to literacy and success at school—for both learners of English and their native English-speaking classmates. More and more, teachers are encouraged to build substantial amounts of vocabulary instruction into the curriculum—in special language classes for learners of English but also in the regular classroom teaching of school subjects such as science, mathematics, and social studies. This book is intended to provide teachers with research-informed guidelines for implementing those objectives.

In this book, we will explore what vocabulary theory and research and the work of educators have to say about teaching and learning second language vocabulary. The goal is to arrive at principled and effective ways of helping primary, middle, and high school students learn the words they need to know. The book is written with learners of English and their teachers in mind, but many of the suggestions will also benefit learners whose home language is English.

Chapter 1 begins with the idea of frequency. It is proposed that the words learners will meet most frequently are the most important to know and that frequency is a useful basis for selecting words to teach. The chapter goes on to detail the nature of vocabulary knowledge. We will see that there is much more to knowing a new word than being able to say, 'Word X means Y'.

In Chapter 2, we explore theoretical and research perspectives on learning words in a second language. These explanations help us understand how word knowledge evolves as child learners attend to the world around them and the language they hear. Theory and research also have a great deal to tell us about classroom word learning activities and teaching techniques that contribute to the retention and effective use of new word knowledge.

In Chapters 3 and 4, we review findings of studies that have investigated the acquisition of second language vocabulary in classroom settings. We look at factors that help and hinder learners' growth. We see that even though their word learning accomplishments are impressive, learners of English often do not know enough of the vocabulary that is critical to their success at school. Practical, research-informed ideas for designing instruction to address this deficit are discussed. The emphasis is on helping learners acquire knowledge of large numbers of new words—through effective teaching, but also through showing them how to become effective autonomous word learners. Chapter 3 focuses on studies done with young learners ranging from pre-kindergarten age to about 11. In Chapter 4, we review studies of learners aged 12 to 18.

Chapter 5 provides a summary of the most important points covered in the earlier chapters.

Chapters 2, 3, and 4 each include two Spotlight Studies; these are more detailed accounts of notable research studies. They have been chosen because of their strong, sometimes unexpected findings which have clear implications for teaching and learning vocabulary. They are also intended to illustrate different ways of answering important vocabulary questions through research. Another recurring feature in this book is the Classroom Snapshot. Most of the snapshots are transcriptions of classroom interactions in which we hear the voices of real teachers and learners. We will hear teachers explaining vocabulary, students volunteering information about words, pairs of learners working together on tasks that make use of new words, and more. Obviously, these cannot capture all of what is involved in implementing an entire research-informed program of vocabulary instruction. They are intended to illustrate the challenges learners face and make the suggestions put forward in this book more concrete. Most chapters also include activities that invite you to test your assumptions or deepen your understanding of research findings. Some of these are simulations; that is, they encourage you to reflect on underlying vocabulary learning principles and possible concerns from the perspective of the teacher or language learner.

There are many excellent resources available for teachers and researchers interested in second language vocabulary acquisition. An annotated list of a few of the sources used in writing this book are found in the Suggestions for Further Reading section. The Appendix provides links to online tools and resources that are discussed in each of the chapters, and the Glossary offers definitions of terms that may be unfamiliar to some readers. Sometimes, a familiar term such as *chunk* has a special meaning in the context of vocabulary studies; such terms also appear in the Glossary. Words defined in the Glossary will be in bold print the first time you meet them in the text; the Index will allow you to find other mentions of them. The References section provides full information for all the sources that are cited in this book.

There is currently a great deal of interest in vocabulary in the research community and in teacher training programs. It is one of the fastest growing areas in second language acquisition research. New technologies have brought innovative ways of investigating vocabulary learning and new kinds of learning activities. For example, researchers can now use sophisticated eye-tracking software to understand the nature of reading in a new language by observing how learners attend to familiar and unfamiliar words in a text. We also know that learners everywhere are increasingly exposed to English language input through digital media—often for many hours a day. The potential for learning new vocabulary through this kind of exposure has only begun to be explored. This book is intended to introduce some of the findings and recommendations for teaching and learning vocabulary that have arisen from research, and to whet your appetite for further exploration of this exciting field.

1
Vocabulary Knowledge and Learning Goals

Preview

The modern English term 'word' stems from an ancient Indo-European root that means 'speak' or 'say'. With this in mind, it seems fitting to begin this book about vocabulary with a conversation. In Classroom Snapshot 1.1, we see a teacher interacting with a group of immigrant learners of English in a conversation about clothing and giving attention to vocabulary along the way. Read the teaching excerpt and consider the words that are given attention and the techniques the teacher uses. Are these important words to know? Do you think the students will remember them? What do you notice about the method of teaching?

Classroom Snapshot 1.1

Adult learners of English in Canada, who come from a variety of first language backgrounds, are discussing shopping for clothing and answering questions based on pictures. The responses designated as 'Student' speech come from several different speakers in the class.

Student: I need some new underwear. I'm going to buy three new underwears.
Teacher: Three new …?
Student: Is it pantyhose?
Student: Pairs.
Teacher: Pairs. Three new pairs today. Okay. Why do we say 'pairs of underwear'?
Student: Two.
Teacher: Okay, two, but why do we say 'pair'?
Student: [unclear response]
Teacher: Top and bottom? No.
Student: There are two feet.
Teacher: Uh huh. Pairs of socks. It's because it's like pants. With pants there's two parts. Right? With underwear, there's not really two parts, but we think there's two parts. There's two holes. So we say 'a pair of underwear'. It's really one part, but we think of it as having two holes. Right?

Student: Also for glasses.
Teacher: Also for glasses, yeah. 'A pair of glasses' because there's two parts, yeah.
[a few interactions later]
Student: Eh, and a tee shirt.
Teacher: Okay.
Student: And a pants.
Teacher: And a pants?
Student: A pair of pants.
Teacher: And a pair of pants.
Student: A pair of pants and high tops, and the laces are open.
Teacher: The laces are not …?
Student: Closed.
Teacher: Tied.
Students together: Tied.
Student: Tied.
Teacher: Or they are unlaced?
Student: Unlaced, yes. And, eh, he has a ball, a basketball.
Teacher: Okay, and what about the shirt? The tee shirt, is it …?
Student: Loose, loose.
Teacher: It's loose. How do we say that?
Student: I don't know.
Teacher: It's not …? It's not tucked in. It's not tucked in.
Student: Tucked in.
Teacher: If your, your mother says, 'tuck in your shirt', your shirt is always untucked.
Student: T-o? T-u?
Teacher: [unclear] Not tucked in or it's untucked. So the shirt's untucked; it's not tucked in. Okay, how about this second lady? She has a wart on her forehead. Linda, how would you describe this second one?
Student: She's wearing a skirt.
Teacher: Yes.
Student: And very high hells.
Teacher: High?
Student: Pair of heels.
Teacher: Heels, yeah.
[a little later]
Teacher: Okay, good. So are there any questions about the clothes?
Student: What's the 'grungy', 'grungy'?

Teacher: Grungy. Grungy. Does anyone know 'grungy'? Grunge means dirt. Grunge means dirt. So, in the early 1990s, you'd see lots of kids walking around with their shirts untucked. Their hair was long and straggly sometimes. They wore big, loose clothes. They wore jeans, maybe with holes in them, and that was the, the grunge movement, era, bunch of people. So they listened to a particular kind of music, and they didn't like to wear very nice clothes.

From unpublished data for a research project led by Laura Collins
(see Springer & Collins, 2008, for more information on the research context)

Readers may wonder whether Classroom Snapshot 1.1 is meant to illustrate 'good' vocabulary teaching. There are definite strengths worth noting. For one, the teacher appears to have a clear sense of which words are probably not well known to her students (*untucked, unlaced*). In the case of *pair*, she skillfully draws out students' existing knowledge of the word and then builds and expands on it with examples. Rather than supplying *tied*, a word she suspects the students know, she gets them to do the mental work of retrieving it. She takes care to present *tucked in* as a two-part lexical chunk and provides a relatable use in context: 'Your mother says "tuck in your shirt".' She is also responsive to her students' questions about words and able to provide a full definition of *grungy* on the spot that connects the word to clothing, music, and the original meaning *dirt*. Making multiple associations gives learners a variety of ways to connect to the word. There are also many useful repetitions of words. For example, in explaining *grungy*, the teachers recycles *untucked*, a word she had explained a few moments earlier. A possible criticism of the teaching is the amount of attention given to an unusual word like *grungy*. By contrast, the attention given to *pair* and its use in the chunk *pair of (two-part things)* seems like time well spent. We sense intuitively that this is language that the students will need to use frequently in everyday life in an English-speaking country. Word frequency and the idea that teaching should prioritize frequent words are topics we will explore in detail later in this chapter. Teaching techniques used in the excerpt and the principles that underlie them will be discussed in Chapter 2.

What is Vocabulary Learning?

Learning new vocabulary is a familiar human activity. We are all aware of encountering a new word and asking someone about it or looking it up online or in a dictionary. We observe young children learning to name objects and persons in the environment around them, and a baby's first spoken word is a memorable event. Vocabulary teaching practices are familiar, too. If you have had the experience of studying a **second language** (**L2**) at school, what do you remember about learning new L2 words? Perhaps you were required to memorize lists of words and their **first language** (**L1**) translations. Maybe you were in a conversation class like the one in Classroom Snapshot 1.1 where words that came up were explained informally along the way. You may also remember keeping a vocabulary notebook. Do you feel you know enough words in your second language to study a school subject in it? You might also try to remember how you learned foreign words that occur in English like *Gesundheit* or *déjà vu*. Were they explained to you? Or did you learn these words through hearing them in use without ever being told exactly what they mean?

Your experiences are likely to affect your views of what vocabulary knowledge is and the teaching and learning methods that work best. As we examine studies of classroom teaching, you will probably discover that many of your intuitions about effective vocabulary instruction are supported by research. But there will likely also be some surprises. Before reading further, take a moment to consider the views you hold using the statements in Activity 1.1.

Once you have arrived at your own judgments, ask others about theirs. If possible, talk to colleagues whose experiences differ from your own and make comparisons. Note your responses and the main points of agreement and disagreement with your colleagues. As you read this book, be on the lookout for information that confirms or challenges the judgments you made here. We will return to these statements in Chapter 5.

Activity 1.1

The following statements reflect views that some people hold about vocabulary knowledge, word learning goals, and teaching methods. Read each statement and check one of the columns to indicate how much you agree or disagree with it.

SA = Strongly Agree   A = Agree   D = Disagree   SD = Strongly Disagree

	SA	A	D	SD
1 In classroom vocabulary teaching, any word that seems unfamiliar to a group of learners is worth explaining.				
2 Secondary school learners of English need to know roughly 5,000 word families to be able to succeed in their studies in mainstream classes in English-medium schools.				
3 Children's first language knowledge has a positive impact on their second language vocabulary learning at school.				
4 Reading stories helps young children learn the academic vocabulary they need for success at school.				
5 Once the teacher has explained a new word, the learner should be able to remember the word and use it.				
6 In teaching a new word, the most important thing teachers can do is explain the meaning.				
7 Once students know the base form of a new word (*grunge* or *lace*, for example), the meanings of the other family members (*grungy, unlaced*) will be obvious.				
8 Understanding the basic meaning of *pick* helps learners of English understand expressions like *pick up a language* and *pick on someone*.				
9 When nine of the words in a ten-word sentence are understood, the meaning of the remaining unknown word can be easily guessed from the others.				
10 Learning new words 'naturally' through reading or hearing them in use is an effective way to learn vocabulary.				
11 Teachers should encourage their students to study lists of words by practicing with word cards (cards with words on one side and pictures, translations, or definitions on the other).				
12 Adolescents learn L2 vocabulary more quickly than younger learners.				
13 Teachers should point out cross-language word resemblances even though the L1 and L2 meanings do not always match up perfectly.				
14 Teachers should train learners in techniques for guessing the meanings of new words.				

Which Words are Important to Know?

To address their students' needs effectively, teachers of English need a sense of which words are the most useful for their students to know. In recent years, computer technology has made it possible to provide a surprisingly concrete answer to this question in the form of lists of frequent English words. The idea underlying a frequency-based approach is that 'general' learners who need to know spoken and written English for a wide variety of purposes are best served by focusing on the words they are most likely to meet and use frequently. *Pair*, for example, is more frequent than *grungy* in English; according to the frequency perspective, this makes *pair* the more useful word to know.

Corpora and Frequent Words

Determining the most frequent words in a language relies on large digital collections of naturally occurring samples of language known as **corpora** (plural form of **corpus**). A corpus should be carefully designed to represent the kind of language it is intended to capture. For example, if the corpus is meant to be representative of spoken language, the designers need to make principled decisions about the kinds of speech to include. Conversations will obviously be an important component, but decisions will also have to be made about the proportions taken up by academic lectures, political speeches, news reports, and so on. Corpora can be specialized; for example, a corpus might be gathered to represent a regional variety of English or a **genre** such as business writing.

Two important general English corpora are the British National Corpus (BNC) and the Corpus of Contemporary American English (COCA); these are available to the public and can be downloaded from the BNC and COCA websites (see Appendix). The BNC and COCA are made up of hundreds of millions of words taken from newspapers, journals, books, and many other written sources; they also include hundreds of millions of words of spoken language. An important feature of a corpus is that it can be searched electronically; search tools can be used to assemble examples of a particular word in use and tally the number of times it occurs in the entire corpus, and whether it occurs throughout the corpus or just in some parts of it. The huge size and representative structure of general English corpora such as the BNC and COCA mean that they provide reliable word frequency information. What is the most frequently occurring word in English? It will probably come as no surprise that it proves to be *the*. More surprising, perhaps, is that the second most frequent word is *of*.

Counting instances of *the* and *of* in a corpus is relatively simple because these two words have no alternate spellings. But determining the frequencies of many English words is complicated by the fact that they have variants formed by the addition of prefixes and suffixes. The word *untucked*, which was highlighted by the teacher in Classroom Snapshot 1.1, is an example. If we want to check a corpus to determine whether *untucked* is a frequent English word worth teaching, what should we search for—*untucked* or the base form *tuck*? It is logical from a pedagogical perspective to consider *tuck* as a single unit or family that includes members such as *tucking*, *tucks*, *tucked*, and *untucked*. We might assume that once learners know *tuck*, they will readily recognize the meaning of the other family members. With this perspective in mind, many vocabulary acquisition researchers use the family unit in their work and define a **word family** as a **headword** and its basic **inflections** and **derivations** (Nation, 2013). Inflections are formed by adding grammatical endings to a headword; in the case of the verb *tuck*, the inflected forms are *tucks*, *tucking*, and *tucked*. Derivations are formed by adding prefixes or suffixes that change the word's meaning or part of speech: adding the prefix *un-* to *tucked* creates an opposite meaning; adding the suffix *-able* creates the adjective *tuckable*. Some frequency lists use the **lemma** unit instead of the family; a lemma is the base and inflected forms of a word only. The lemma *work* includes *works*, *worked*, and *working*, but not derived forms like *worker*, *reworked*, and *unworkable*. This book will use the more inclusive term 'family'. However, the pedagogical assumption underlying this choice is not without its problems. It may be safe to assume that learners who know *crime* will understand *crimes*, but will they also understand *decriminalization*? We will return to this point in Chapter 3.

With a working definition of 'word family', we can return to the question of whether *untucked* is useful to know in terms of its frequency in the English language. The question can be answered by entering it into a **lexical frequency profiler**. This computational tool allows the user to enter single words or longer passages; the software then classifies each entered word according to 1,000-family frequency lists (or lemma-based lists) that are derived from corpora. The online profiler VocabProfile is available on the Lextutor website (see Appendix). Another widely used profiler is AntWordProfiler, available on Laurence Anthony's website (see Appendix). Lexical frequency profiling reveals that *untucked* and the rest of the *tuck* family are found on the list of the 4,000 most frequent English word families (according to lists by Nation, 2012, based on the BNC and COCA). This makes *tuck* what Schmitt and Schmitt (2014) have termed a mid-frequency family. As we will see, it is important for learners beyond the most basic levels of proficiency to know mid-frequency vocabulary, so the time spent explaining *untucked* in Classroom Snapshot 1.1 can be seen as a good investment. By contrast, the *grunge* family is not found until the 11,000-level list, which confirms that *grungy* is a low-frequency word and not a very good investment in terms of its overall usefulness.

Coverage

Word frequency is closely tied to the idea of **coverage**. Frequent words are useful to know because they account for, or 'cover', a great deal of the vocabulary found in samples of written and spoken language. Coverage research shows that a surprisingly small number of words makes up the majority of the running words in any continuous stretch of language. With knowledge of only the 10 most frequent word families of English, readers will be familiar with almost a quarter of all the words they meet in typical written passages (Nation, 2001). If the 100 most frequent families are known, coverage increases dramatically to almost half. But these are mostly function words like *the*, *of*, *have*, and *you*, and while knowing them is obviously important, there is clearly a limit on what can be expressed or understood with knowledge of just these 100 families.

The picture becomes more interesting once learners of English know all of the 1,000 most frequent word families. With this knowledge, three quarters (or more) of the written words they encounter in their reading will be made up of familiar vocabulary. Spoken language has been shown to rely more heavily on frequent words than writing, so even more of what they hear will be familiar. With knowledge of the 2,000 most frequent word families, coverage increases further still from 85% to as much as 90%, depending on the genre (Nation, 2006). These 2,000 word families are clearly very important for learners of English to know.

Recently, Schmitt and Schmitt (2014) have made strong pedagogical arguments for increasing the number of 'must-know' words to the 3,000 most frequent word families. Adding 1,000 more families boosts known-word coverage to as much as 95%. Schmitt and Schmitt point out that makers of monolingual learner dictionaries typically draw on 2,000 to 3,000 high-frequency word families in writing definitions, so knowledge of the 3,000 most frequent word families should enable learners to understand the words used to define entries in those dictionaries. In addition, the 3,000-level list contains many important academic words that are used to explain abstract concepts in school textbooks. They also point out that 3,000 is a manageable figure: designing instruction to promote the acquisition of this number of families is a large but still feasible undertaking.

To get a sense of the importance of knowing the 3,000 most frequent word families in English and its relevance for reading at school, consider the following multiple-choice question taken from a high school science exam administered in Canada. The text has been altered to reflect how it would appear to a hypothetical learner of English who knows only the 1,000 most frequent word families (along with numbers and symbols like °C). The blanks in the text represent words that would not be known. The known words represent 73% of the total number of words, but is it readable in your view?

1,000 word families
A group of students _____ an _____ to _____ the _____ of _____ on _____ rates. They _____ three _____ _____ in this _____. In the first _____, they drop an _____ _____ into a _____ of water at a _____ of 40°C and record how long it takes the _____ to completely _____.
In the second and third _____, they use the same type and amount of _____, but they change the _____ of the water to 25°C for the second _____ and 5°C for the third _____.

Question: Which _____ is _____ in the _____?
A the kind of _____ used in the _____
B the _____ of _____ used
C the _____ at the time of the _____
D the amount of time needed for the _____

Perhaps you were able to discern that the passage pertains to a basic scientific experiment. But it seems clear that the learner taking this exam would find the test question impossible to read and answer. The version that follows next is the same as above but with the 2,000-level word families added. Here, we assume the reader knows the 2,000 most frequent word families (plus numbers and symbols). Adding the 2,000-level word families brings the proportion of familiar words up to 84%. How does this version compare in terms of comprehensibility? Is it now possible to answer the test question?

2,000 word families
A group of students _____ an _____ to determine the effect of _____ on reaction rates. They perform three separate trials in this _____. In the first trial, they drop an _____ _____ into a _____ of water at a _____ of 40°C and record how long it takes the _____ to completely _____. In the second and third trials, they use the same type and amount of _____, but they change the _____ of the water to 25°C for the second trial and 5°C for the third trial.

Question: Which variable is _____ in the _____?
A the kind of _____ used in the reaction
B the _____ of _____ used
C the _____ at the time of the reaction
D the amount of time needed for the reaction

Opinions will vary, but it seems safe to say that this version is considerably more comprehensible. It attests to the usefulness of knowing the 2,000 most frequent English families. That said, the text is still not easy to read and much remains unclear. Next, we turn to a version of the text that assumes a learner with knowledge of the 3,000 most frequent families. With the 3,000-level word families added, the known-word coverage is 92%. How does this change impact comprehensibility in your view? Can you guess the meanings of the missing words?

3,000 word families
A group of students conducts an experiment to determine the effect of temperature on reaction rates. They perform three separate trials in this experiment. In the first trial, they drop an _____ _____ into a _____ of water at a temperature of 40°C and record how long it takes the _____ to completely _____. In the second and third trials, they use the same type and amount of _____, but they change the temperature of the water to 25°C for the second trial and 5°C for the third trial.

Question: Which variable is manipulated in the experiment?
A the kind of _____ used in the reaction
B the quantity of _____ used
C the temperature at the time of the reaction
D the amount of time needed for the reaction

We can probably agree that this version is more comprehensible. Studies consistently show that L2 readers of English need to understand at least 98% of the words in a reading passage in order to perform adequately on a measure that tests comprehension of the passage (Nation, 2006). That is, with two unfamiliar words embedded in a context of 98 familiar words, it becomes possible to understand the text reasonably well and perhaps successfully guess the meanings of the unknown vocabulary. Some successful guessing also appears to be possible with 95% coverage, but it is less reliable. Here in the 3,000-level version, the known-word coverage is 92%—just under the 95% criterion—but you were probably able to correctly infer that something was dropped into a container of water in the third line. In the full original text which appears below, we can see that one of the words missing in the third line of the 3,000-level text is *beaker*. While uncertainties remain, with knowledge of the 3,000 most frequent word families, the L2 learner is in a substantially better position to understand the passage, guess the meanings of some of the unknown words, and answer the question correctly (the correct answer is C).

> **Original**
> A group of students conducts an experiment to determine the effect of temperature on reaction rates. They perform three separate trials in this experiment. In the first trial, they drop an antacid tablet into a beaker of water at a temperature of 40°C and record how long it takes the tablet to completely dissolve. In the second and third trials, they use the same type and amount of antacid, but they change the temperature of the water to 25°C for the second trial and 5°C for the third trial.
>
> Question: Which variable is manipulated in the experiment?
> A the kind of antacid used in the reaction
> B the quantity of antacid used
> C the temperature at the time of the reaction
> D the amount of time needed for the reaction

Deciding Which Words to Teach

Frequency offers a principled basis for deciding which words are most deserving of deliberate teaching attention and which the teacher should attend to minimally or leave for learners to study on their own. Schmitt and Schmitt (2014) have devised a scheme that divides general English vocabulary into high-, mid-, and low-frequency zones, and suggest how classroom teachers should deal with words in each of these zones. Decisions about the words to teach obviously also depend on the needs of individuals or groups of learners and their proficiency level. Our discussion in this book focuses mainly on the needs of school-age English language learners (ELLs). ELLs are minority-language students who are acquiring English in a school setting where English is the majority language. A typical example is a Spanish-speaking student in a primary school classroom in the United States. In this consideration of which words to prioritize, we will also discuss **academic vocabulary** and the specialized **domain-specific vocabulary** that are found in school textbooks.

High-Frequency Vocabulary

High-frequency words are defined as those that appear on lists of the 1,000, 2,000, and 3,000 most frequent word families (Schmitt & Schmitt, 2014). These are important words to know, and teachers and textbooks should ensure that ELLs have good opportunities to learn them all. Some L2 vocabulary researchers see equipping learners with knowledge of the 2,000 most frequent words as a pedagogical imperative. Meara (1980), for example, proposes that school language programs simply put all else aside and target the learning of 50 words per week for 40 weeks in the first year. Nation (2001) is no less emphatic: with reference to the 2,000 most frequent families, he observes that high-frequency words are so important that anything teachers and learners can do to make sure they are learned is worth doing. Learning activities for high-frequency words should involve listening, speaking, reading, and writing skills. In addition to practice in meaningful contexts, learners also benefit from studying the words in isolation using word cards (Gardner, 2013) or word games (Cobb & Horst, 2011). Simplified literacy materials such as **graded readers** are a useful way of providing learners with repeated reading encounters with high-frequency words. Graded readers are simplified classic novels or original books designed to give learners interesting content to read without burdening them with difficult vocabulary.

As we have seen, high-frequency words are of crucial importance because of their great coverage. The example of the science exam question given earlier demonstrates their coverage of written language; these words also play a powerful role in covering spoken **discourse**. The lists of the 1,000, 2,000, and 3,000 most frequent word families discussed here are based on the BNC and COCA. The BNC and COCA lists of the 1,000 and 2,000 most frequent word families are also referred to as the Common Core List (CCL) (Gardner, 2013). An older but still useful list of 2,000 frequent word families is the General Service List (West, 1953). (These lists and other vocabulary resources discussed in this book are available on the Victoria University of Wellington website; see Appendix.)

Mid-Frequency Vocabulary

Earlier in this chapter, *untucked* was identified as a **mid-frequency** word. Mid-frequency vocabulary is defined as words found on the lists of the 4,000 through 8,000 most frequent word families (Schmitt & Schmitt, 2014). The decision to end the mid-frequency range at 8,000 word families is based on an important study by Nation (2006) entitled 'How large a vocabulary is needed for reading and listening?' He found that knowledge of around 8,000 word families is needed to ensure that L2 readers have known-word coverage of many types of written language at the 98% level. The study also found that spoken language (as represented by the script of a movie and a corpus of transcribed conversations) requires knowledge of 6,000 to 7,000 word families.

Designing courses or materials to systematically teach all of the thousands of words in this very large range is challenging. Nonetheless, time spent teaching mid-frequency words is a worthwhile investment because of their role in making the authentic written and spoken discourse of native speakers accessible to learners. Since there is probably not enough time in class to teach all these words, learners may need to work on them on their own. The teaching of word learning strategies is important in this regard. Students can be shown how to use knowledge of word parts to understand and remember new words, how to guess meanings of words from context, and how to use word cards for effective review (Nation, 2013). Teachers do well to have a sense of the mid-frequency words that occur in classroom materials so that they can highlight them when they come up in class. Lexical frequency profilers make it easy to identify the mid-frequency words in a textbook passage. The lexical profilers mentioned earlier in this chapter, such as VocabProfile and AntWordProfiler, have been designed for this very purpose.

Low-Frequency Vocabulary

What should teachers and learners do about **low-frequency** vocabulary? As the descriptor 'low' suggests, these are words not found on the lists of high- or mid-frequency word families. Any word on the 9,000-level list or beyond is classified as low-frequency (Schmitt & Schmitt, 2014). *Lollapalooza, fastigiate,* and *aviatrix* are examples of some very infrequent words (from the 25,000-level of BNC- and COCA-based lists). Generally, language teachers should not devote class time to teaching low-frequency words simply because they are not very useful to know. Nation (2013) makes this point using a financial metaphor: spending time and effort on words with low-coverage value amounts to a poor investment. That said, a quick explanation of a low-frequency word is warranted if students need to understand it in order to proceed with an activity. As they become more proficient, learners will need to know some low-frequency vocabulary. But since there are tens of thousands of low-frequency words, developing classroom activities to systematically teach them all is unfeasible. Rather than spending valuable class time on low-frequency words, teachers can more usefully help learners develop guessing strategies and skill at using both printed and online dictionaries so that they can determine the meanings of the low-frequency words they meet on their own.

How should teachers respond if students have questions about low-frequency words, as in the case of the student in Classroom Snapshot 1.1 who asked about *grungy*? Given its low frequency (11,000 level), we might judge that the teacher spent too much valuable class time explaining it. However, before judging her too harshly, we should recognize that we do not know much about the circumstances of the explanation. If the student who asked the question had previously expressed a special interest in fashion and music, the detailed answer about the grunge movement seems justified. We can hardly fault the teacher for responding to her students' interests!

Academic Vocabulary and Domain-Specific Words

Researchers have also set out to determine whether it is possible to identify academic vocabulary that would be useful to learners in educational settings. They ask the question: Is there a vocabulary of school? In the first two years of primary education, the answer appears to be no. The language young native speakers of English encounter at school tends to resemble the everyday spoken language in the home. This puts young ELLs who have little exposure to English at home at a distinct disadvantage as they attempt to learn to read; they must cope with **decoding** written representations of English words that may be unfamiliar to them (Geva & Ramírez, 2015). However, the vocabulary of school changes in an important way around the time children reach Grade 4. At this stage, school texts begin to focus on facts and information that are not expressed in the language of a child's everyday experience. Chall (1996) notes that at this point, school reading shifts from 'learning to read' to 'reading to learn'. Children in Grade 4 and beyond are expected to read and understand texts on topics such as the structure of the solar system, factors leading to World War II, and the differences between mammals and reptiles. Coping with this new kind of reading is a challenge for both native L1 English speakers and ELLs. Knowledge of the academic vocabulary found in such **expository** text is identified as an important factor in successful school reading from Grade 4 onwards (Chall & Jacobs, 2003). Learners also need to use academic vocabulary in their speaking and writing.

The term 'academic vocabulary' has a specialized meaning in the field of vocabulary studies. Academic vocabulary words are the general, non-technical (or 'sub-technical') words used to explain concepts and link them together in meaningful statements. Examples of academic words are *define*, *process*, *sequence*, *minimal*, and *factor*. The term does not refer to domain-specific words like *mammal* and *reptile*. Following a bricks-and-mortar metaphor devised by Dutro and Moran (2003), words like *mammal* and *reptile* are the vocabulary bricks that represent the substance of an academic subject (biology, in this instance). Academic words function as the mortar that joins the bricks. For example, in a textbook passage that compares mammals and reptiles, we can imagine meeting words and phrases like *contrast*, *similarity*, and *major difference*.

The words *contrast*, *similarity*, and *major* are found on the **Academic Word List** (**AWL**), an important list developed by Coxhead (2000). The AWL is made up of 570 academic word families that occur frequently in university reading across a variety of subjects. It is based on a 3.5-million-word corpus of university textbooks representing 14 different subject areas. Analyses indicate that knowledge of the AWL word families offers readers of academic texts a substantial known-word coverage boost (Coxhead, 2000). We can see this in the test question about a simple science experiment we examined earlier in this chapter: one word in every 15 is an AWL word. The AWL is widely recognized as a useful list for school reading and writing and many books and online learning activities are available to support it. The list is available for download on the Victoria University of Wellington website (see Appendix). The Academic Vocabulary List (AVL) is another useful resource. It is a newer list of academic words based on a much larger corpus of 120 million words of academic text developed by Gardner and Davies (2014); it contains 3,000 frequently used lemmas. The AVL is available on the Academic Vocabulary List website (see Appendix).

> **Activity 1.2**
>
> Some researchers have questioned whether an all-purpose, non-specialized academic vocabulary really exists (Hyland & Tse, 2007). They point out that some AWL words have meanings that are specific to the discipline in which they are used. For example, *volume* and *analyze* have different meanings in science, commerce, and the humanities. To explore this issue, consider the AWL words that occur in the test question about the simple chemistry experiment discussed earlier in this chapter. They are *conduct, manipulate, occur, reaction,* and *variable*.
>
> 1 Imagine that these words were used in a review of a musical performance. How do the meanings change?
> 2 How would they change if they occurred in a business report?
> 3 In your view, does this issue invalidate the concept of an all-purpose, cross-disciplinary academic vocabulary?
> 4 What implications does it have for teaching academic words? For example, how would you explain the meanings of *reaction* and *variable* to learners of English?

Why are we discussing lists of academic words based on university reading materials in a book that targets the vocabulary needs of young learners and adolescent learners of English? Since knowledge of academic words is important for studying at the university level, it makes sense for teachers to ensure their students know these words by the end of high school. In addition, academic families found on the AWL occur frequently in the language of the textbooks that upper-primary, middle school, and high school students are expected to be able to read at school.

The AWL has proved to be a reasonably good guide for work with adolescent learners, but there is now a newer corpus-informed list that is specific to the needs of middle school learners. The **Middle School Vocabulary Lists (MSVL)** developed by Greene and Coxhead (2015) are made up of AWL and other academic word families that occur frequently in textbooks used by middle school students. To make the lists, Greene and Coxhead created the Middle School Content-Area Textbook Corpus, an 18-million-word collection of 109 textbooks used by students in Grades 6, 7, and 8 in public schools in the United States. The corpus was divided into five sub-sections based on subject matter: 1) English grammar and writing, 2) health, 3) mathematics, 4) science, and 5) social studies and history. Analysis of the most frequently occurring word families in each section resulted in five sub-lists of roughly 400 families each. There is overlap between one sub-list and another. For example, *affect* occurs in the health, science, and social studies lists. The division into subject sub-lists helps ensure that learners become aware of meanings specific to a particular subject. For instance, the word *volume* occurs on all five sub-lists including the mathematics list; this indicates that the teaching of *volume* should raise learners' awareness of its mathematical meaning as well as the meanings relevant to the other subject areas.

The test question we examined earlier (see page 13) contains seven words from the MSVL's science sub-list of 435 word families. One word in every 12 in the question can be found on this list, an even higher level of coverage than the one-in-15 coverage provided by the AWL. Although this coverage finding is based on just one short passage, it suggests that the MSVL provides a very useful set of words for school-age learners to know. If middle school learners know the 2,000 most frequent English word families and the families on the MSVL, about 90% of the words they meet in their school reading in the five subject areas will be familiar (Greene & Coxhead, 2015). The MSVL is available on the Lextutor website (see Appendix).

Understanding classroom content and learning new concepts at school clearly also involves learning domain-specific or 'brick' words. If the topic is animal biology, for example, teachers will need to give attention to words such as *reptile*, *mammal*, *vertebrate*, and *species*. However, this is often precisely the vocabulary that is already well supported in textbook materials through pictures, in-text explanations, and highlighted definitions. Because they are the main focus of a content-area lesson or unit, teachers may be inclined to attend to these domain-specific words and overlook the abstract, and sometimes rather colorless, academic words that are so crucial to understanding explanations of concepts and links between ideas (Dutro & Moran, 2003). Domain-specific words are sometimes also referred to as technical, specialized, or Tier 3 words; you may come across these terms in your reading.

Activity 1.3

Locate a passage from a science or social studies textbook your students use, or look for a stretch of expository text online. A good search term is 'science news'; any non-fiction text will do. The passage should be about 100–150 words in length. Read through the text and underline the words that you think can be classified as academic vocabulary. Note that you are looking for words like *define, process, structure,* and *factor*. Then, highlight the words you think can be classified as domain-specific.

Go to VocabProfile (VP-Classic) on the Lextutor website (see Appendix) and check your predictions by entering the text into the 'main text' window. Be sure to remove the instructions from the window before you paste in your text. Select the MSVL option and then click 'Submit'. In the output, you will see the percentages of words in the 1,000-level, 2,000-level, and MSVL categories. Scroll down to see a color-coded version of the text. The MSVL words (the academic vocabulary) will appear in yellow. Scroll further to see which of these are on the science sub-list of the MSVL. Words that appear in red are 'off-list'; that is, they are not 1,000-level, 2,000-level, or MSVL words. Words you identified as domain-specific vocabulary are likely to be found in this category.

1 How well do the results match your predictions?
2 What percentage of the text is accounted for by MSVL words?
3 Note the percentages accounted for by 1,000-level, 2,000-level, and MSVL words taken together. How close would knowledge of these words bring the reader to the 98% coverage level that research suggests is needed to understand the text without dictionary assistance?
4 Did anything surprise you? How do the findings affect the way you think about the vocabulary in the passage and what your students need to know?
5 Try the same analysis using the AWL option. What differences do you notice?

Which Word List?

Many vocabulary lists intended for use with learners of English as a second language are available. How can teachers identify the one that is right for their students? The perspective taken in this book is that vocabulary lists informed by large corpora that reflect the language ELLs need to know are the most useful. They offer high levels of coverage of general and school language not found with lists that do not make use of corpus information. An important set of well-designed frequency lists derived from the BNC and COCA (Nation, 2012) has been mentioned often in this chapter. The

BNC and COCA lists have been specially created with learners of English in mind and have several features that make them a useful set of lists for many general language teaching purposes. They reflect both spoken and written English sources, and have been calibrated to overcome the heavy influence of formal written text that is normally characteristic of large native-speaker corpora. The use of both British and American sources is intended to decrease regional bias. The AWL and MSVL are also corpus-informed. These frequency lists based on textbook corpora make them highly suitable for use with learners who need to know the written language of school.

Teachers may be familiar with other useful word lists that are not corpus-based, such as A List of Essential Words by Grade Level (Marzano, Kendall, & Paynter, 2005), Academic Vocabulary List (Marzano, 2002, 2004), Waystage (Van Ek & Trim, 1991; see Appendix), and Threshold (Van Ek & Trim, 1990; see Appendix). These lists are based on expert judgment, close examination of school materials or policy documents, or by compiling and updating earlier non-corpus-based lists. Another list, Words Worth Teaching (Biemiller, 2010), is based on investigations of the words learners know at various grade levels. These various lists include some of the same words found on the corpus-based lists discussed in this chapter. However, they are unlikely to be able to match the coverage of well-designed corpus-based frequency lists. Analyses by Greene and Coxhead (2015) bear this out: they found that the non-corpus-based lists they investigated offered far lower coverage of middle school textbooks than their MSVL.

Large corpora and powerful computational tools have greatly enlarged our understanding of the English language in ways that have direct implications for language teaching. This discussion has focused on identifying the general and academic words that are most useful for school-age ELLs to know, but there are other important uses of corpora. For example, a corpus can be searched to identify frequently occurring combinations of words (*sort of*, *a bit of*) or the verbs most likely to take complement clauses (I *think* that ..., I *know* that ...). Such patterns of co-occurrence may be difficult for humans to detect but are easily identified using corpus tools (O'Keeffe, McCarthy, & Carter, 2007; Reppen, 2010). Researchers continue to create new corpus-informed frequency lists. The lists mentioned in this chapter as suitable for use with ELLs will no doubt eventually be replaced by improved versions. This section has emphasized the usefulness of a corpus-informed approach to vocabulary teaching but ends with the reminder that humans are needed to implement it. Frequency lists can tell us that *variable* and *volume* are important academic word families, but teachers help to make the words memorable for learners. Specific suggestions for teaching academic vocabulary are discussed in Chapters 3 and 4.

Dimensions of Vocabulary Development

What kinds of things can learners do with words as their vocabulary knowledge grows? In this section, we explore three dimensions of learners' developing L2 lexical ability. The discussion expands on ideas originally put forward by Henriksen (1999). First, we consider the 'partial–precise dimension' (p. 304).

Partial to Precise Knowledge

Classroom Snapshot 1.2 shows how a teacher draws on her students' knowledge to bring the class from a vague and incomplete notion of a word to a much more precise understanding of its meaning.

> **Classroom Snapshot 1.2**
>
> Ms Jenkins (all names are pseudonyms) reads a newspaper article regarding a recent poll of public opinion about the US President with her fourth-grade class. She stops to pose a question: 'What does *popularity* mean?' The room is silent for a few moments as the 9- and 10-year-olds put their minds to work. Antonio, a student known more for the frequency of his answers than their accuracy, raises his hand. 'It's like something about the President.' 'OK,' Ms Jenkins notes, 'Can anyone add to what Antonio said?'
>
> Ms Jenkins faces a sea of furrowed brows and blank stares. She glances at the clock on the wall and begins to wonder if they will make it through the text before lunch. After a long silence, Brenda responds. 'It's what the people think about the President, like how much they like him,' she suggests. 'Great, Brenda. You're right, how did you figure that out?' 'Well,' Brenda pauses. 'I looked at it for a while, trying to find a word inside it that I do know like you told us to do last week, and I found the word *popular*. A popular kid is, you know, a kid that people like, so I figured that *popularity* must have to do with that.' 'Good work, Brenda, in attacking that word to find a part that you know. Did anyone try something different?' After a longer pause, Rafael raises his hand. 'Well, I did what Brenda did. But when you say *popular*, I think of Spanish, and it's *como popular*. And when on television they say *el Presidente es popular*, it means they like him.'
>
> (Kieffer & Lesaux, 2007, p. 134).

Henriksen (1999) proposes that the process of learning a second language begins with an awareness that the word exists, but knowledge of its meaning is initially uncertain and imprecise. Antonio's response in Classroom Snapshot 1.2, 'It's like something about the President', is indicative of this early stage.

The idea that there are various levels or stages of lexical knowledge is captured by the Vocabulary Knowledge Scale (VKS), a measurement instrument developed by Paribakht and Wesche (1997, p. 180). Test takers are asked to report their knowledge of a tested word according to the following scale:

---
1 I don't remember having seen this word before.
2 I have seen this word before, but I don't know what it means.
3 I have seen this word before and I think it means _____ (synonym or translation).
4 I know this word. It means _____ (synonym or translation).
5 I can use this word in a sentence. For example, _____ .

It is worth noting that not every instance of L2 word learning will progress neatly through each of the five phases along the continuum. For example, French-speaking learners of English might realize very quickly that *flower* is equivalent to *fleur* in their mother tongue and never really go through the imprecise phases represented by Levels 2 and 3. This appears to be the case with Rafael in Classroom Snapshot 1.2, who has realized that *popular* has a similar form and meaning in English and Spanish. Forgetting and relearning occur as well; that is, a learner might reach Level 4 for a given word but then regress for a while to Level 3 or Level 2 (Horst & Meara, 1999). The point to note here is that knowledge of a word is usually partial and imprecise at the outset and then develops gradually towards a more fully delineated and accurate sense of the meaning.

An example from research by Horst (2009, p. 48) illustrates this incremental growth. At the beginning of the study, one of the participants, a Spanish-speaking adult learner of English, reported that she did not know the word *van*. Later, after reading two graded readers in which *van* occurred a total of five times, she was tested using a measure similar to the Vocabulary Knowledge Scale described above. She responded as follows:

Definition: *van* = the back of a big car
Example: We put a lot of things in the <u>van</u> when we go in holidays.

The student clearly had gained partial but imprecise knowledge of the word. She correctly identifies it as a noun and assigns a meaning associated with motor vehicles. After 17 weeks of continued exposure to English, the student was tested again. This time she responded as follows:

Definition: *van* = 1) A big car, 2) the back of the car
Example 1: This week-end I am going to travel to Quebec City in my brother's van.
Example 2: Put all of these big things in the back of the van.

As the first definition and example indicate, her knowledge of *van* has become more accurate. However, it remains partial; she has not yet rejected the incorrect meaning. The idea that L2 vocabulary knowledge is acquired incrementally over the course of meeting new words many times is a consistent theme in L2 vocabulary acquisition research; it has been confirmed over a wide variety of learning contexts (Nation, 2013; Schmitt, 2008). We will take a closer look at the process of learning vocabulary through repeated encounters in Chapter 2.

The partial–precise dimension has several implications for instruction. When teachers single out words that come up in class activities, they are doing the important work of initiating the word acquisition process. Some of the vocabulary highlighted in Classroom Snapshot 1.1 got only a moment's attention, but the teacher lifted the words out of the stream of communication in a way that said, 'Here is something to attend to'. Even though the learners may not remember very much about these words, they begin to be aware that they exist. The idea of incremental progress along a scale like the VKS also serves as a reminder to not expect too much too soon from students as they learn new vocabulary. Once new words have been explained in class, teachers often ask the students to use them correctly in meaningful sentences of their own, a task that represents the most advanced knowledge state on the scale (VKS Level 5). This may be very challenging for learners who are meeting these words for the first time. Under pressure, they may produce vague sentences that reveal very little understanding, such as 'I saw the *flower*'.

Depth of Knowledge

The second dimension in Henriksen's scheme is depth of knowledge. **Vocabulary depth** can be defined very generally as 'the quality of the learner's vocabulary knowledge' (Read, 1993, p. 357). If knowledge of a word is deep, the learner can do more than provide a single definition or translation of words like *flower* or *van* (VKS Level 4). Deep knowledge entails the ability to use the words in more complex ways such as incorporating them into **semantically** and grammatically accurate sentences (VKS Level 5). Arguably, there should be a Level 6 on the scale that would be indicative of knowing a word in even greater depth. Deeper knowledge of *flower* would entail knowing that it is both a noun and a verb; that the suffix -*y* can be added to form *flowery*; that it is associated with other words like *fragrance*, *tulip*, and *vase*; and that it occurs in collocations such as *flower garden* and *flower pot*. Knowledge at Level 7 might include awareness of the 1960s Flower Power movement, customs like flower girls at weddings in Western culture, metaphors involving flowers (*the flower of one's youth, wallflower*), and many other expanded uses. We will take a much closer look at the various kinds of knowledge that contribute to deep word knowledge later in this chapter.

Receptive and Productive Knowledge

The third dimension is the receptive–productive continuum. **Receptive knowledge** (also known as 'recognition knowledge') has to do with understanding words when they are heard or read, while **productive knowledge** has to do with putting words into active use. Receptive knowledge normally precedes production; that is, learners usually understand L2 words before they use them in speaking or writing. The receptive-to-productive sequence is reflected in the VKS, where the first levels (1, 2, 3, and 4) all pertain to understanding a new word while the last and highest level (5) involves productive knowledge.

The term 'receptive' is apt in that a stimulus is received. By way of illustration, consider the word *exit*. If a learner hears or reads the word *exit* in 'The exit is on the left', and is able to make the connection to the mental concept of 'way to get out, door leading out', the learner can be said to know the word receptively. Productive knowledge comes into play if the learner wants to express the meaning communicated by our example sentence. Is the learner able to fill in the gap in 'The _____ is on the left'? In other words, productive knowledge of a word means being able to supply the spoken or written L2 form that matches the concept the learner has in mind. In this case, successful productive processing involves searching the mental **lexicon** for the English word form that means 'door leading out'; and once *exit* has been recalled, the learner then says or writes it. The idea that productive knowledge builds on receptive knowledge is supported by research showing that L2 learners' receptive vocabularies are consistently larger than their productive ones (Nation, 2013; Waring, 1997). Some L2 words may never be learned productively; this applies to L1 vocabulary as well. For example, you may understand the word *egregious*, but it may not be a word that you ever actually say. It is interesting to consider whether there are exceptions to the receptive-to-productive sequence: Is it possible to have productive knowledge of a word for which one does not have receptive knowledge? Children's use of swear words which they do not fully understand is one example; other examples might include words in nursery rhymes or religious language.

Meaningful production of L2 words is cognitively more demanding than reception for a number of reasons. Both processes involve mental effort, but producing a spoken word requires the added effort of articulation. Reception may also be easier than production simply because we have more experience of it; we hear and read much more than we say and write (Nation, 2013). The idea that production is more challenging than reception has relevance for classroom review of vocabulary. Since L2 learners will be able to answer questions that require receptive processing more easily than those that require production, the review of recently taught words should begin with recognition questions. For example, the teacher can ask, 'Which one means "door leading out"—*exit* or *ticket*?' A question that requires production like 'Do you remember the word that means "way out"?' can come later once the students are more familiar with the word.

In this book, the terms 'receptive' and 'productive' will be used, but some writers and researchers use the terms 'passive' and 'active'; you may encounter these alternate terms in your reading. It is true that vocabulary production can be characterized as active: the L2 learner is called upon to recall and deliver a spoken or written word. But characterizing the receptive aspect as passive is problematic. As anyone who has tried to learn a new language knows, the act of listening and trying to understand the words in a rapid stream of foreign language speech requires a great deal of mental effort and can hardly be described as passive. Reading in a foreign language is also demanding and researchers have found that even skilled readers usually need more time to understand a text written in their second language than they need for reading in their L1. Favreau and Segalowitz (1983) suggest that this is at least partly due to the fact that second language readers have to put more effort into comprehension because there are words that they are not (yet) able to understand automatically in a way that native English-speaking readers, who have seen the words many more times, are able to do.

The three knowledge dimensions—partial–precise, depth of knowledge, and receptive–productive—offer a useful way of thinking about learners' vocabulary development. But in real L2 word learning, these are not separate entities. Instead, we can envision the dimensions as processes that are supportive of each other. For example, we can imagine a scenario where understanding words and concepts in the context surrounding a new word like *van* (the depth dimension) might move knowledge of the word from an imprecise understanding of its meaning to a more accurate sense (the partial–precise dimension), and that this knowledge would support the learner's ability to eventually use the word productively (the receptive–productive dimension).

Components of Vocabulary Knowledge

Teachers and learners often see the meaning of a word as the main aspect to understand and remember. In fact, there is a great deal more to know. Various aspects of word knowledge have been outlined in a comprehensive framework by Nation (2013); a modified version based on work by Hedgecock and Ferris (2018, p. 125) appears in Table 1.1 (Activity 1.4; see page 30). As learners come to know words in the ways described in the framework, they are developing deep vocabulary knowledge. In the first column of the table, we see that word knowledge is divided into three main aspects: form, meaning, and use. Each of these is divided into the three components shown in the second column. In the third column each component is operationalized by asking two questions. The first addresses receptive knowledge (R) while the second pertains to productive knowledge (P). Before we explore the various components in more detail, you are invited to see how the scheme works for yourself in Activity 1.4.

Form

Learning to recognize and produce the form of a new word is more difficult than it may seem. Acquiring knowledge of the sounds and spelling of words can be challenging for L2 learners. For one thing, the forms of words are arbitrary, and this makes them difficult to remember. In the case of the word *bug*, for example, there is no logical reason why a *b* sound is associated with the bug concept in English. Nor are any of the other sounds or letters in the word particularly bug-like. Most learners of English will already be familiar with the bug concept, so the meaning aspect is relatively unproblematic. The challenge is to learn and remember the unfamiliar string of sounds and sequence of letters that constitute the new L2 label for this known concept.

Activity 1.4

Answer the questions in the third column for the word *disability*. Since the word *disability* has already been provided, the receptive questions marked *R* are more relevant than the ones marked *P*.

Main aspect	Components	Clarifying questions
Form	spoken	R: What does the word sound like? P: How is the word pronounced?
	written	R: What does the word look like? P: How is the word written and spelled?
	word parts	R: What parts (roots, prefixes, and suffixes) are recognizable? P: What word parts are needed to express this meaning?
Meaning	form and meaning connection	R: What meaning does this word form signal? P: What word form can be used to express this meaning?
	concept and referents	R: What is included in the concept? P: Which word(s) can be used to refer to this concept?
	associations	R: What other words does this word make us think of? P: What other words could we use instead of this one?
Use	grammatical functions	R: To what grammatical category/categories does this word belong? P: In what grammatical patterns must we use this word?
	co-occurrence	R: With what other words or types of words does this word occur? P: What words or types of words must we use with this one?
	constraints on use (register, frequency)	R: Where, when, and how often are we likely to meet this word? P: Where, when, and how can/should we use this word?

Table 1.1 Components of Vocabulary Knowledge

Reflect on your experience. Which aspects were confusing or difficult to respond to? Are some aspects more important than others in your view? Which do you think learners would find the most difficult to acquire? Also consider how complete the framework is. Can you think of aspects of word knowledge that are not captured by this framework?

This relabeling task is cognitively demanding, but it is simpler than the work young children must do as they acquire the vocabulary of their first language. For them, both the concepts and the labels are new and unfamiliar.

Children who learn an L2 at a young age tend to have native-like pronunciation of words. Research confirms the 'earlier is better' relationship for pronunciation; the mental capacity for acquiring pronunciation in a natural, child-like manner appears to diminish as learners reach adolescence. The more accurate pronunciation of young children may also be due to opportunities to learn and practice without the pressure to perform that older learners may experience (Lightbown & Spada, 2013). For older L2 learners, acquiring the spoken form of a word is affected by the closeness of its sounds to the sounds of their L1. Thus, the difficulty that L1 Japanese speakers may experience in pronouncing English words can be ascribed at least in part to the fact that Japanese does not have some of the vowel and consonant sounds used in English. Many studies show that words which are difficult to pronounce are harder to remember. Experiments with non-words bear this out. For example, English speakers will find a non-word that has familiar sound combinations (*blard*) more memorable than one that does not (*pzugw*). Studies also show that L2 learners tend to avoid using words that are difficult to pronounce (Laufer, 1997).

Awareness of the letter–sound correspondences of English, which L1 learners may not develop until about the age of six, is helpful in sounding out new words and spelling them (Webb & Nation, 2017). If L2 learners have learned to read in an L1 that has an **alphabetic system** and uses the Roman alphabet, they may be able to apply this ability to pronouncing new English words. In alphabetic languages such as French, Dutch, and Spanish, letters correspond to sounds. But since the letter–sound correspondences of these languages differ in some ways from those of English, learners with these L1s must learn to associate some familiar letters with new sounds. For example, French *quitter* does not sound much like *quitter* in English. Learners whose L1s do not use the Roman alphabet system clearly face a large challenge, as they must learn a new **orthography** or even an entirely different system of representing language. Arabic-speaking learners of English must learn both a new orthography and a system that represents vowels more fully than is usual in written Arabic. Even the idea of connecting sounds to letters may be new for some learners. Mandarin Chinese, for example, is not alphabetic; it uses characters to represent entire semantic concepts. English words are notoriously difficult to spell because the sound–symbol correspondences are not always predictable. The letter *g*, for example, represents different sounds in *good, gentle, mirage,* and *gnat*; the sound of *f* has different spellings in *rough, staff* and *pharmacy*. These irregularities present spelling and decoding challenges for L1 and L2 learners alike. Geva and Ramírez (2015) provide a detailed account of how young readers overcome these difficulties as they develop their L2 reading skills.

The third component of the Form section in Table 1.1 is 'word parts'. This pertains to the roots, prefixes, and suffixes that make up a word, and is also known as **morphology**. Learners need to be able to see that a word like *readjustment* consists of the root form *adjust*, a prefix *re-*, and a suffix *-ment*. It is obviously helpful if they know that *re-* means 'again' and that *-ment* is a noun maker. Much of the Greco-Latin vocabulary of English makes use of prefixes and suffixes that have close counterparts in Romance languages. For example, both Spanish and French use *re-* as a prefix meaning 'again'. Speakers of these languages therefore have an advantage when it comes to learning the morphology of English words. Some learners may also be aware of the Latin roots in a word like *adjust* (*ad* = to, *just* = near). In addition to recognizing the forms and meanings of word parts, learners need to be able to produce **affixed words**. Thus, full knowledge of the verb *adjust* means being able to say and write related forms like *adjustor, adjusting,* and *readjusted*. Acquiring knowledge of the affixes that can and cannot be added to a particular root word is an attested challenge for adult L2 learners of English (Schmitt & Zimmerman, 2002). The difficulty may be explained by the absence of rules; the verb *adjust* requires the noun-making suffix *-ment*, but there is no logical reason why another noun-maker like *-ation* or *-ance* cannot be used instead.

Children acquiring English as their L1 generally know the inflections of English words (plural *-s*, *-ed* past, *-er* comparative, and so on) before they start school. Their ability to recognize prefixed and suffixed words has been shown to grow dramatically at school, especially during the third, fourth, and fifth grades. The burst in growth is ascribed to the development of morphological problem-solving skills, which continue to increase in sophistication throughout the high school years (Hancin-Bhatt & Nagy, 1994). Studies confirm a close connection between awareness of word parts and overall vocabulary knowledge in primary learners (Ramírez, Chen, Geva, & Luo, 2011).

Meaning

The first component in the Meaning section of Table 1.1 is 'form and meaning connection'. This refers to the ability to make a link between the form of a word and its meaning at the most basic level: X means Y. The number of words that learners can recognize and associate with a simple definition is referred to as their **vocabulary size**. Speed is not mentioned in the table, but fluent L2 listening, speaking, reading, and writing all depend on the ability to make form–meaning and meaning–form connections very quickly for a large number of words. Developing rapid lexical access or **automaticity** is a topic we will return to in Chapter 2. Sometimes a form–meaning connection can be established relatively easily. For example, in the case of a Spanish speaker who encounters the English words *popular*, *explosion*, and *festival* for the first time in a reading passage, making the connections can happen almost immediately because all three are spelled the same way in Spanish and have similar meanings in both languages. If the words were met in a listening context, they might not be so easily recognized, since they do not sound exactly the same in Spanish and English. Nonetheless, it is clear that the cognitive burden of linking new L2 words to meanings is lighter in cases where there are formal resemblances to familiar L1 words with similar meanings.

L2 words that are formally similar to words in a learner's L1 are **cognates**. For example, English *mother* and German *Mutter* can both be traced back to the same ancient Germanic root and an even older Indo-European ancestor. Formally similar L1–L2 word pairs can also be explained by the borrowing of words from one language into another. English has a long history of borrowing vocabulary from Latin, Greek, and French; these **loanwords** are often familiar in form and meaning to speakers of Romance languages. The English word *flower* (French *fleur*, Italian *fiori*, and Spanish *flor*) from Latin *florem* is an example. English continues to borrow words from other languages. Recent borrowings such as *sushi*, *burrito*, and *cappuccino* may be familiar to many learners of English because of their use internationally.

The 'concept and referents' component in Table 1.1 refers to awareness of the various meanings of **polysemous** words; these are words with several related meaning senses. An example is the word *bug*. It is defined as 'insect', but there are several extended meanings related to the idea of an irritating or harmful creature. The noun form can refer to an electronic listening device placed with malicious intent, an irritating computer glitch, or an illness caused by a harmful bacterium or virus. The connection to the idea of an irritant is also evident in its use as a verb (to bother someone or place a listening device). Learners with this extended knowledge of a word's meaning are aware of its various senses and can recognize the intended meaning of *bug* in a sentence, such as 'We want to make sure there is no bug in the system'. Hedgecock and Ferris (2018) include **pragmatics** in the 'concept and referents' component. Knowledge of pragmatics involves an understanding of the social context in which it is appropriate to use a word (or other language feature). We can see *bug* as a word we might use rather informally, in speaking to a child, for example.

The third component, 'associations', may be familiar from the **word maps** that teachers often use to show links between associated words (these are also known as 'semantic maps' or 'word webs'). If we imagine the word *bug* in the center of a word map on a whiteboard, one type of associate that a teacher may try to elicit from students (and add as nodes on the map) is words for kinds of bugs they may be familiar with—*bee, mosquito, ant,* and so on. Other types of associate are synonyms, such as *insect* and *pest,* and words related to the larger group that bugs belong to, such as *animal* and *creature*. Words related to the attributes of bugs—*wing, fly, bite, sting, crawl*—are also associates. Antonyms (opposites) are another type of word associate.

Use

Knowledge of a word also involves knowing the company it keeps. In Table 1.1, this is referred to as 'co-occurrence'. In the case of *bug*, native speakers of English know that *bug* can be paired with *stomach* to form the familiar expression *stomach bug*. They also know implicitly that *bug* cannot be paired with *foot* or *head* in the same way. Other terms for words that commonly occur together include **collocation, multi-word unit, formulaic sequence,** and **chunk**. Examples are *get married, drop like flies, look up* (in a dictionary), and *strong coffee*. Although researchers do not always agree on definitions for these terms, some general characteristics can be identified (Laufer & Waldman, 2011). Formulaic sequences are combinations that are distinct from ordinary free language use: 'Let's *look up* that word (in a dictionary)' differs from from '*Look up* at the clouds' in this way. There is also some restriction on the elements that can occur together. For example, we can say *strong coffee,* but we do not normally say *powerful coffee* (even though it is grammatically correct). Finally, the meanings of chunks may be difficult to interpret from the meanings of the constituent words. While *get married* seems relatively transparent, the meanings of *stomach bug* and *drop like flies* would probably need to be explained to a learner of English. Being able to access memorized multi-word chunks contributes to making speech fluent. That is, when a speaker can produce a long phrase like 'The fact of the matter is …' fairly effortlessly as if it were a single word, this frees up mental resources to work on the parts of the message that are not pre-constructed (Pawley & Syder, 1983).

Learners who are new to English certainly know the usefulness of memorized phrases like 'Could you please repeat that?' and 'Excuse me'.

Formulaic sequences are known to be an area of difficulty for learners of English. Comparisons of large collections of learners' speech or writing (**learner corpora**) to native-speaker corpora consistently show that L2 learners produce fewer formulaic sequences overall and their use is less varied. Laufer and Waldman (2011) found that even very advanced adult learners underused collocations in their writing. When they were used, errors like *bring examples* and *learn children* (instead of *give* and *teach*) were common and could often be ascribed to L1 influence. Inaccurate production of formulaic sequences may also be explained by the arbitrary nature of the chunked words; there is no logical reason why *take a step* is correct and native-like, while *do* or *make a step* is not.

The 'Use' section in Table 1.1 also includes knowing the grammatical functions of words. As we have seen, *bug* can function as either a noun or a verb when used in a sentence. Full knowledge of the grammatical functions of this word entails being able to use it as a noun and as a transitive verb that can operate on an object—the *me* in 'Don't bug me'. The final component in Table 1.1 speaks to constraints on the use of a word and refers to **register**, which pertains to the style or tone the speaker or writer is seeking to achieve. We can probably agree that *bug* is an informal word rather than a scientific one. Intuitively, it feels like a word that we would be more likely to say than write, and a corpus comparison based on the BNC written and spoken sections bears this out: the *bug* family is used twice as often in speech as it is in writing. It is also worth noting that register is closely allied with frequency, because unusual words tend to sound more formal than common ones.

Since Nation published his version of this table in 1990, it has been cited many times. It is an important contribution because it illustrates how large and multifaceted the task of learning new L2 vocabulary is, and it raises our awareness of aspects of knowledge that might be easily overlooked. While explaining the meanings of new words is obviously important, instruction that helps learners develop knowledge of forms and uses is important, too. In Classroom Snapshot 1.1, the meaning of the word *pair* was clearly explained, but over the course of the activity, it was also said aloud at least nine times—sometimes by the teacher and sometimes by the students—almost always in contexts that featured the collocation *pair of (something)*. If any students were able to use *pair* more accurately after this class, what made the teaching effective? The repeated exposure to the form, the repetition of the collocation pattern, or the explanation of the meaning? The interplay of all three of these factors is likely to have been important.

The framework explored in Activity 1.4 (see page 30) is a useful taxonomy, but it is not a lesson plan. A single vocabulary lesson could not target all nine components of vocabulary knowledge; nor could students remember all the information. As we have seen, knowledge of new vocabulary develops incrementally as learners hear, see, and produce a word repeatedly over time. The framework is not a vocabulary syllabus either. Though some of the more difficult components are closer to the bottom of the table, it is not meant to be used as a teaching sequence that begins with practicing spoken forms and ends with instruction on register constraints. The different aspects are not acquired independently; rather they are learned in parallel with knowledge of one component supporting the development of the others.

Summary

In this chapter, you were invited explore your views of vocabulary and to reflect on your experiences of learning and teaching new words. Corpus-based frequency lists were introduced as a principled way of determining the words that are the most useful for learners of English to study. We looked more closely at the vocabulary needed to succeed in school, which differs substantially from the everyday vocabulary of conversation. We also considered the paths vocabulary knowledge follows as it evolves and examined the components that contribute to deep knowledge. As we have seen, there is a great deal more to know about a word than just its meaning! In Chapter 2, we will see what theories of word learning can tell us about the factors that contribute to effective L1 and L2 vocabulary learning at home and at school.

2 Learning Vocabulary

Preview

In this chapter, we explore theory and research relevant to learning vocabulary. The concepts, frameworks, and research findings presented here serve as a backdrop to the classroom vocabulary studies discussed in Chapters 3 and 4. We begin the chapter with a brief look at early word learning in child vocabulary acquisition and the challenges that young L2 learners face. We then explore theories that address the important question of how vocabulary knowledge is acquired and retained. We also discuss ways of applying theoretical concepts and research findings to teaching and learning vocabulary in classrooms, with particular attention to school reading and academic words.

Setting the Scene

Word learning is a labeling task. As young children seek to understand the world around them and attend to the language they hear, they begin to form concepts and to map words and phrases onto these concepts. Early L1 word learning may seem 'natural' and effortless, but the challenge should not be underestimated. For instance, we can imagine a child who hears various speakers use the word *dog* in contexts that involve a stuffed toy, a picture in a book, a cartoon on television, and a visit from a real cocker spaniel. The child is faced with identifying features of the 'dog' concept that are shared across these very different contexts. The fact that the child will probably also hear other words such as *play*, *bark*, *pat*, *quiet*, *nose*, *tail*, and *Don't be afraid* used in the same contexts adds to the complexity of the task. The child must eventually also determine what exactly is included in the 'dog' concept and what is not. Initially, the concept may be over-extended and applied to other animals. Under-extension is also possible; the child may not use the word *dog* for a chihuahua, which is not a prototypical 'doggy dog' (Aitchison, 1994; Clark, 1993). As more words become known, children become more able to use the semantic contexts surrounding the new words they hear; that is, they can use the words they know to infer new word meanings, and vocabulary acquisition proceeds more quickly (Dockrell, Braisby, & Best, 2007; Tomasello, 2003).

Children who have substantial exposure to two languages in the years before they reach school age are referred to as **simultaneous bilinguals**. They acquire the vocabulary of both languages through attending to the language input they are exposed to in much the same manner that monolingual children acquire L1 vocabulary. Children who first meet a new language at school, after they have developed considerable L1 knowledge, are referred to as **sequential bilinguals**. They are clearly in a different position since their L2 vocabulary learning begins at a point when some L1 vocabulary is already in place. According to the **interdependence hypothesis** proposed by Cummins (1979), a child's level of L1 language ability before encountering the L2 at school plays a substantial role in supporting the development of L2 proficiency at school. The relationship has been confirmed in many studies and it makes sense: having a great deal of L1 vocabulary knowledge in place means that children already have a large store of named concepts in their mental lexicons, and L2 word learning becomes largely a matter of applying new labels to concepts that are already known (Cummins, 1979; Paradis, 2007). Thus, L1 vocabulary development supports L2 vocabulary development, which in turn supports learners' ability to use the new language. Recent confirmation of this connection comes from research that has found a strong association between productive oral vocabulary skills in L1 Spanish in kindergarten and reading skills in English in the early primary years (Kieffer, 2012).

Spotlight Study 2.1 was one of the first studies to look closely at the vocabulary learning of young Spanish–English bilinguals in the United States. At the time, there was a concern that learning two languages simultaneously might mean that neither language is learned very well.

Spotlight Study 2.1

Umbel, Pearson, Fernàndez, and Oller (1992) compared the vocabulary knowledge of bilingual first graders in their two languages—Spanish and English—using picture recognition tests. Some of the learners were simultaneous bilinguals who had been exposed to both Spanish and English at home before they entered school; others were sequential bilinguals who were first introduced to English at school.

Performance in both groups on the test of Spanish vocabulary was near the established norm for monolingual Spanish speakers. Exposure to English at home or at school had not 'damaged' their Spanish. The researchers also found that the simultaneous bilinguals scored higher on the English test than the sequential group. Since the simultaneous bilinguals had more exposure to English before they started school, this outcome is not surprising. Although the learners did not score as high as the established norm for monolingual native speakers of English on the English vocabulary test, the study shows that all of the young L2 learners were able to grow their vocabularies in two languages at the same time. So concerns that learning two languages at once might be harmful to vocabulary development in one or the other are unfounded. Indeed, developing and maintaining knowledge of two (or more) languages over time has been shown to offer cognitive advantages (Bialystok, 2007).

The findings are encouraging in that we see that exposure to the majority language (English) did not result in a great loss of the home language (Spanish). The researchers note that this is hardly guaranteed; minority children from less advantaged families may have much less well-developed L1 skills than the middle-class children that were investigated in this study. The research highlights the importance of encouraging families to support their children's L1 development, as this lays a foundation for their L2 development at school.

Theories of Vocabulary Acquisition

How is second language vocabulary acquired? In this section, we will examine several important theories that offer research-informed explanations of how first and second languages are learned. The theories are wide-ranging and address many aspects of language acquisition; our discussion will focus mainly on what they can tell us about learning vocabulary. Why is it important to think about theory? Theories can provide teachers with a fuller understanding of the learning process, enabling them to support their learners' development in many principled ways that go beyond simply explaining new words in class.

Behaviorist Perspectives

An influential theory of language learning in the 1940s and 1950s was **behaviorism**, a perspective championed by Skinner (1957) in the United States. At the heart of this perspective is the basic principle that language is learned through imitation and positive reinforcement. Traditional behaviorists hypothesized that children learned their first language through reproducing words or phrases they heard in the language around them, and that 'rewards' for good imitations—in the form of parental praise or the satisfaction of communicating successfully—moved acquisition forward (Lightbown & Spada, 2013). In language teaching, the audio-lingual approach implemented behaviorist principles in that L2 learners repeated simple grammatical sentences and dialogues many times, with a view to developing good language 'habits'. A few new words were introduced in these drills, but only enough to make the drills possible; more attention was given to mastering the grammatical patterns and reproducing accurate pronunciation (Zimmerman, 1997). In the 1960s and 1970s, behaviorism lost ground to views of language acquisition that focused more on children's ability to discover the structure of the language they heard. The language of developing L1 learners was shown to not be strictly imitative (Bloom, Hood, & Lightbown, 1974), and linguists were consumed by Chomsky's (1959) revolutionary ideas about the brain's capacity for acquiring linguistic knowledge that went beyond what was explicitly available in the environment. In the 1970s and 1980s, language teaching methods that centered on the development of L2 knowledge through meaning-focused communicative interaction became popular, and behaviorism-inspired drilling and repetition came to be seen as overly mechanical and artificial.

In these developments, the focus was largely on the acquisition of grammatical features; how a large vocabulary might be acquired was not given much consideration (Schmitt, 2000; Zimmerman, 1997). More recent theoretical frameworks (discussed below) give vocabulary acquisition a far more central role, but also reflect some of the characteristics of behaviorism. More specifically, there is a renewed interest in 'old-fashioned' repetition and memorization techniques because of their usefulness in developing automatized word knowledge. Increasingly, researchers recognize the importance of having multiple opportunities for **retrieval**. Receptive retrieval occurs when a learner sees or hears a word and recalls its meaning. Retrieval can also be productive; that is, the learner has a concept in mind and recalls the word form needed to express the meaning (Webb & Nation, 2017). Each experience of a successful retrieval strengthens the form–meaning connection in the learner's mind; many retrievals may be needed before the mental connections can be made rapidly (Baddeley, 1990). Deliberate rehearsal of words and definitions using a list or a set of word cards with words on one side and their definitions on the other is a useful way of learning new vocabulary through multiple retrievals. Research by Elgort (2011) shows that word knowledge gained in this way is not as static or limited as might be expected. She found that the new vocabulary learned through studying word cards became well integrated into L2 learners' mental lexicons, and could be accessed in a manner similar to the way learners draw on existing L1 and L2 lexical knowledge in real language use. Retrieval activities need not be boring; popular word games often involve repeated opportunities to recall forms or meanings. There are now many apps and online programs for word-card study available. These include Quizlet, Memrise, Anki, VTrain, and Lextutor flashcard builder (see Appendix).

The Usage-Based Perspective

Rehearsal with word cards is one way of learning vocabulary through multiple retrievals, but in fact the world of real communicative language use abounds with opportunities for lexical retrieval. Words and phrases are heard in conversations and learners must make mental connections to their meanings. When words or phrases are unfamiliar, the physical and linguistic environment can offer clues to meanings. The idea that children develop language knowledge through the experience of attending to language and the environment around them is central in **usage-based theory** of first and second language acquisition. Usage-based theory posits that children's early language acquisition is shaped by their remarkable ability to perceive patterns in the language they are exposed to, together with a strong drive to communicate with others (Tomasello, 2003). Experiments show that, well before they are able to speak, babies can recognize a repeated string of nonsense syllables, even if they have heard it only once before (Saffran, Aslin, & Newport, 1996). Though they are highly attuned to frequently used words and phrases, their first words are not *the* and *of* (the most frequently occurring words in English), but words like *mama* or *more*, which are used to draw attention or communicate need. These early words reflect a developing understanding of what language is used for as well as sensitivity to frequently heard language.

In explaining how language learning occurs, proponents of usage-based theory point to the cumulative effects of thousands of experiences of associating words with elements in the learner's environment. Thousands of experiences of hearing words used with other words and phrases are also critical. The usage-based perspective is closely aligned with **connectionist theory**, which has used computer simulations to investigate the role of frequency effects in associating words with other words and phrases. We can imagine that presenting a computer program with many examples of sentences that contain the words *dog* and *bark* but no (or very few) sentences with *dog* and *meow* could eventually result in the computer 'knowing' that a new sentence with *dog* is far more likely to contain *bark* than *meow*. The example is hypothetical, but if we apply it to all of the words, phrases, and sentences that a human language learner hears over years of exposure, we can see that learning via a basic associative mechanism could eventually result in a vast mental network of lexical, collocational, and grammatical associations. Although the hypothesized learning mechanism is relatively simple, the knowledge that arises out of thousands of associative experiences is complex. Usage-based theorists see basic associative learning as an explanation for the acquisition of other complex abilities in young children, such as learning how to interpret the visual world; it is not only specific to language learning (Ellis, Römer, & O'Donnel, 2016; Ellis & Wulff, 2015; Tomasello, 2003).

There is abundant evidence to support the idea that L2 learners acquire words they meet in the language input they are exposed to, and that meeting words frequently makes form–meaning connections stronger. Testing using corpus-based measures that sample word families of various frequencies shows a broad overall frequency effect across a wide variety of L2 learning contexts. That is, learners' performance is best on the part of the test that assesses knowledge of word families that are very frequent in the language at large and learners' scores are progressively lower as the frequency of the tested families decreases. Individual learner profiles do not always follow this pattern, possibly due to the particular type of exposure the individual may have had (many hours spent with chemistry textbooks, for example). But the performance of groups indicates that learners tend to acquire words in an order that quite closely reflects how often the words are likely to be met in the language input to which they are exposed (Milton, 2009). We will return to the effects of meeting new words frequently in the discussion of reading later in this chapter.

Studies of child vocabulary acquisition indicate that the main explanation for differences in the vocabulary sizes of preschool children is simply the amount of language they hear in interaction at home (Biemiller, 2003). Almost all of the words that preschool children produce are words they have heard their parents use (Hart & Risley, 1995). A famous study that links parent talk to their children's vocabulary development, and makes the connection to reading performance later at school, is described in Spotlight Study 2.2.

Spotlight Study 2.2

Hart and Risley (2003) created preschool programs designed to boost the vocabularies of children in poverty, but they were concerned about the effectiveness of the interventions. They found that the programs succeeded in teaching the preschoolers new words; but when they reached kindergarten, the vocabularies of the less advantaged children still lagged well behind those of more advantaged children and their growth was slower. In other words, the vocabulary knowledge gap between the advantaged and less advantaged children was large and becoming ever greater. To better understand the source of the problem, the researchers decided to see what was happening to children at home at the very beginning of their vocabulary growth.

They observed interactions between children and parents in 42 families for an hour each month over a period of more than two years. All of the language that each child was exposed to during the hour of observation was recorded and transcribed. The children were less than a year old when the monthly observations started; once they began to talk, their speech productions were also recorded. The families continued to be observed until the children reached the age of three. Based on the occupation of the parents, the researchers divided the families into three income groups: professional, working class, and welfare families.

The authors were astonished and saddened by the differences the data revealed. In the professional families, children heard many more words than in the less advantaged groups. The amount of parent talk the children were exposed to was mirrored in the productive vocabulary sizes of the children by age three, and the differences were dramatic. Children in the professional families had an average vocabulary size that was over twice as large as that of the children in the less advantaged families. The researchers wondered what would happen when the children went to school. Six years after the original study was completed, they tracked down 29 of the 42 families and explored the children's school performance. The children were now nine or ten years old and in the third grade. The researchers found that the disparities remained. In fact, vocabulary at age three proved to be a surprisingly strong predictor of language skills at school.

The researchers then used the hourly counts to estimate the average number of words the preschool children had heard at home in all of their first four years before entering kindergarten. The extrapolations indicated that children in the families where amounts of parent talk were low experienced a huge shortfall in comparison to children in families where parent talk was abundant—a difference possibly on the order of 30 million words. It is not without reason the authors titled their study 'The Early Catastrophe'.

This is just one of many studies that identify the connection between low **socioeconomic status** (SES) and deficits in vocabulary development and reading achievement at school in both L1 and L2 learners (Biemiller, 2003). The gap between advantaged and less advantaged children becomes ever wider over the school years as children with impoverished vocabularies struggle with school reading.

Information Processing

Insights from cognitive psychologists working with **information-processing** models of learning help explain how learners eventually become able to access word knowledge automatically. At the center of the information-processing perspective is the idea that the mind has processing limitations. Only so much information can be handled at once; if a cognitive task is highly demanding, fewer mental resources are available for tackling other tasks. According to this account, the learning process begins when a learner becomes aware of and pays attention to a novel aspect of language (DeKeyser, 1998; Schmidt, 2001). As beginning learners read or listen to L2 input, they may be so overwhelmed by the stream of language and so focused on understanding the overall meaning that many linguistic features go unnoticed. Eventually, however, they may notice unfamiliar words. Their attention may be drawn to an unknown word because it has been repeated many times or because it is key to understanding the message of a conversation or text. Learners may also notice that they are missing words that are needed to complete something they wish to express (Nation, 2001; Swain, 1985). Textbook passages often highlight difficult words in bolded type or provide definitions alongside the passage; these features contribute to making words noticeable. Looking up a word in a dictionary or completing a textbook vocabulary exercise involves **noticing**. Words may be noticed because the teacher has singled them out for attention. L2 acquisition research has investigated the effects of **integrated form-focused instruction** (Spada & Lightbown, 2008). This term refers to contexts where, in the midst of communicative classroom interaction, the teacher draws attention to a word (or other linguistic feature). This might take the form of noting the word's importance, offering a definition, or correcting a learner's misuse of a word. Hulstijn and Laufer (2001) have emphasized the motivational component in attending to new words; they hypothesize that learner-generated attention to a word is more likely to result in eventual learning than teacher- or task-imposed attention. Classroom Snapshot 2.1 provides an example of learner-generated attention to new words.

Classroom Snapshot 2.1

Learners can help each other notice words in interactive tasks. Read the following transcript of a problem-solving discussion involving intermediate-level adult ESL learners in New Zealand. The task, which comes from Ur (1981), is about redesigning a pictured plan of a zoo to put all the animals in the best places. Which words appear to be noticed for the first time?

S3: … All enclosures should be filled.
S2: Enclosures should be filled … enclosure, do you know?
S1: What means enclosure? Do you know?
S3: Close, ah … should be filled.
S2: No, I don't know enclose … enclosed.
S1: Filled … what means fill? Oh, oh, all enclosed, I think that all enclosed that means enclosed.
S2: Fill.
S3: Filled, filled.
S2: Ohh.
S1: Every, every area, yes, should be filled.
S2: Should be filled.
S3: Should be put … put something inside.
S1: Yes, because … yes, yes, because you know two? The-
S2: I see. No empty rooms, ahh.
S3: No empty rooms, yeah.
S2: Two is the empty. I see.
S1: Yeah, empty … so we must fill it. OK.

One of the criteria on the task sheet reads, 'All the enclosures should be filled'. In the article from which this excerpt was taken, the authors emphasize the importance of ensuring that task sheets for such activities include some unfamiliar words like *enclosure* and *fill* so that they can be noticed and clarified through negotiation (Joe, Nation, & Newton, 1996).

In the exchange in Classroom Snapshot 2.1, the word *enclosure* was attended to because it was needed to complete the activity; as a result, the learners may have formed a mental association with its meaning. The amount and kinds of attention given to a new word can vary a great deal. The amount may be very slight. For example, we can imagine that while reading a story about monsters, a young learner of English notices the unfamiliar word *huge*, decides to ignore it, and simply reads on. Alternatively, the learner may pause to consider the meanings of the other words in the context surrounding *huge*, look at a pictured monster in the book, recall other monster stories, and then correctly infer that the meaning of *huge* is *big*. The learner may then go on to notice that *huge* looks like *hug*, wonder how to pronounce *huge*, think of its L1 translation equivalent, picture other big things, register the position of the written word on the page, or remember a bad dream with giant monsters. Making such associations is referred to as **elaborative processing**. Cognitive psychology research shows that when new information is first met, the number and quality of elaborations are important in facilitating learning and retention (Anderson, 1990). Richly elaborated processing contributes to making a new word memorable by providing multiple mental pathways for retrieving the word. If one pathway does not lead to the word, another one may—if not the monster picture, then perhaps the formal resemblance to *hug* will lead to the recovery of *huge*. Each additional pathway increases the chances of successful retrieval.

Full 'deep' knowledge of a new word is elaborated knowledge, and for this reason teachers do well to draw learners' attention to the spelling, pronunciation, collocations, morphological variants, multiple meanings, and other aspects of new words (Webb & Nation, 2017). But language learners can hardly be expected to attend to all these aspects in single vocabulary-teaching events. Similarly, we can imagine that L2 readers who are focusing on understanding a reading passage might not have sufficient cognitive resources available to infer the meanings of all the new words they meet and to connect them to other words and experiences in rich and varied ways.

Barcroft (2002, 2009) has looked closely at the effects of processing limitations in acquiring specific aspects of L2 knowledge. His **type of processing–resource allocation (TOPRA)** model hypothesizes that using cognitive resources to work on one kind of learning reduces the amount of attention available for attending to another aspect. In an investigation of TOPRA predictions, Barcroft (2009) asked Spanish-speaking learners of English to read a passage that contained infrequent English words that the learners were unlikely to know along with their L1 translations. Some of the learners were also asked to write another Spanish synonym for each target word; this task meant that their attention was focused closely on the meanings of the new words. A sentence from the experimental passage with blanks for the Spanish synonyms reads as follows (p. 103): 'His co-worker Bob, on the other hand, is just the opposite. Bob is *brash* (descarado _____) and filled with *conceit* (vanidad _____).' Performance on a spelling test given after the reading activity showed that learners who had read the passage without the synonym task were substantially better at providing accurate or near-accurate spellings of the target words. Reading without the synonym task was also associated with better performance on a measure of text comprehension. We can assume that, as TOPRA predicts, these learners had more cognitive resources available to attend to the written forms of the new words and the overall meaning of the passage than those whose attentional resources were depleted by the synonym task. Even though the synonym-producers may have been involved in useful cognitive work, the task detracted from their ability to do other important kinds of processing.

Other investigations of cognitive resource allocation show that, when the goal is to acquire knowledge of the formal characteristics of new words (their pronunciation or spelling), learning activities that focus learners' attention on other formal aspects—such as thinking of a rhyme—are more conducive to the acquisition of formal characteristics than exercises that focus on semantic knowledge, such as studying definitions or using the new words in meaningful sentences (Barcroft, 2002, 2009). These findings are consistent with studies of **transfer-appropriate processing** (**TAP**). According to this principle, newly learned information is best retrieved when the performance conditions resemble the original learning conditions. For example, we can expect students who have practiced writing new words to be more able to spell the words correctly than students who studied the words in another kind of activity. TAP effects are explained by research showing that when we learn something new, we also create associations with features of the context in which the learning took place and the thinking processes we engaged in. These connections are helpful later when we are called upon to access the newly acquired knowledge (Lightbown, 2008).

It is important to note that the findings of processing-allocation studies do not mean that teachers should avoid meaning-focused vocabulary activities. Indeed, the effectiveness of learning new words through semantic elaboration is one of the most robust findings of cognitive psychology research. However, processing-allocation research provides a useful reminder to avoid overwhelming learners with more information than they can handle when they first meet new vocabulary. TAP also reminds us to relate teaching methods to expected outcomes. For example, if we want learners to be able to produce the forms of words, we need to involve them in activities that focus on this aspect, such as oral repetition, picture naming, spelling games, and finding rhymes.

Information-processing perspectives emphasize the role of practice in the development of rapidly accessible word knowledge. Like other kinds of learning, the acquisition of word knowledge is hypothesized to begin with **declarative knowledge**, which is knowledge that we are aware of and can articulate. For example, an English-speaking learner of French might have knowledge of a word that can be stated as: 'I know that *oeuf* in French means *egg* in English.' The use of mnemonics is also declarative in nature; thus, a learner of English might consciously connect a new word to a known word in a reminder like: 'To remember *huge*, I should think of *hugging* a giant monster.' With practice, declarative knowledge can become **procedural knowledge**, which is the ability to understand and use words like *oeuf* and *huge* without having to consciously translate or think of a reminder. With continued practice over the course of many, varied opportunities for retrieval, procedural word knowledge becomes more automatized. Eventually, recognition of the meaning of a word (or phrase) becomes so automatic that the listener cannot help but understand it the instant it is seen or heard. Similarly, the complex process of speaking (choosing words, pronouncing them, and stringing them together) becomes automatic and the conscious translation stage is long forgotten. When word knowledge has become automatized, it can be used without making the large demands on mental processing capacity that processing new information requires, allowing the language user to more easily attend to the overall meaning of a text or conversation, or speak without hesitation. In other words, automaticity underlies what we understand as fluent language use—both receptive and productive. Automatic processing also helps make new learning possible. As L2 learners become more able to use familiar language automatically, they have more cognitive resources at their disposal for activities such as noticing unfamiliar words and inferring their meanings (Segalowitz, 2010).

Noticing, Retrieval, Elaboration

In this section, we take a closer look at three concepts introduced in the discussion of theories of vocabulary acquisition that have direct applications to classroom teaching. These are noticing, retrieval, and elaboration.

We have seen that noticing can happen in a variety of ways. It can be learner-generated: new words may be noticed as learners read or listen to language input, or they may notice gaps in their knowledge as they try to express themselves. Facilitating this kind of noticing in classrooms means creating opportunities for learners to read and listen to materials they can readily understand. Importantly, the materials should contain some new words that are available for noticing but not so many that comprehension is difficult; we will return to this point later in the chapter. There should also be opportunities for output; these are speaking and writing opportunities that involve learners using the language that they know. Production pushes learners to discover gaps in their word knowledge (Swain, 1985). We have also seen that noticing can be promoted in more explicit ways. Textbook vocabulary exercises, teacher explanations, and interactive tasks that engage learners in clarifying words for each other all draw attention to new vocabulary. The common thread is that in order to notice new words, learners need to be able to allocate attentional resources to them. That is, noticing requires putting aside other cognitively demanding activities such as attending to the meaning of the incoming stream of language—however briefly—to give conscious attention to a new word. This idea that noticing requires learners to decontextualize words sheds a positive light on classroom practices such as oral repetition of words or copying words the teacher has written on the blackboard. These 'boring' activities contribute to learning by promoting noticing, though they are clearly only the first step in a much longer learning process.

Noticing a new word is hardly a guarantee that it will be remembered. Once learners become aware of new vocabulary, they need multiple opportunities for retrieval of word forms and their meanings to consolidate their knowledge. The key principle underlying retrieval is 'search': the learner sees a word form and must do a mental search for the meaning, or the learner has a meaning in mind and searches for the appropriate word form. The word cards mentioned earlier are useful tools for practice involving retrieval—for individuals or whole classrooms. Research indicates that the format need not be elaborate; cards with L2 words on one side and simple L1 translations on the other are very effective (Nation, 2013). Word cards may also include definitions in the L2, pictures, examples of the word in use, additional meanings, and other information. Practice with word cards should be done in both directions; that is, learners should look at a meaning and try to retrieve the word form and also look at meanings and try to recall the forms (Nation, 2013).

Opportunities to retrieve previously noticed words need to occur before they are forgotten; research suggests that it is useful to review new words with learners soon after they are first encountered (Nation, 2013). Classroom review activities play an important role in ensuring that learners retain the vocabulary the teacher has explained previously. A good way to end a class is to review the vocabulary that has been highlighted during the lesson; a teaching assistant or a designated student can be given the task of making a list of words that were explained. Words also need to be reviewed repeatedly; once is not enough. Research suggests that this aspect of vocabulary acquisition may be neglected: in a study of transcribed classroom teacher talk, Horst (2013) found that, over a period of nine weeks, only a small proportion of the many words the teacher drew attention to in class were reviewed.

In reviewing words with learners, teachers can optimize opportunities for retrieval by ensuring that the information about previously explained words is not too readily available. For example, if the teacher asks the class, 'Who remembers the word that means X?' and then quickly confirms the correct response volunteered by the most knowledgeable student, the opportunity for the rest of the class to engage in the cognitive search has been shut down. Many more learners can be engaged in retrieval if instead the teacher says, 'Raise your hand if you remember the word that means X, but don't say it yet'. If only a few hands are raised, she can give more clues to the meaning until more hands are raised and the correct response is eventually provided (Nation, 2001). As many learners as possible should be given a chance to try to recall new words.

Another kind of opportunity for retrieval is offered by retelling activities. Learners can be asked to read a text, then put it aside and reconstruct it orally with partners. Revisiting a text in this way engages them in recalling the new words they have just met. Often, the push to move ahead with new classroom content means missing the valuable opportunities for retrieval inherent in reworking and reviewing old material (Webb & Nation, 2017).

So far, we have emphasized the importance of repeated retrievals of the same form–meaning connections—as they might occur on word cards, for example, or in reviewing words that were explained in class. Providing opportunities for retrieval in new meaningful contexts is an important next step. For example, learners can be asked to supply previously studied words in fill-in-the-blank (cloze) exercises that present new sentence contexts for the words. This more demanding kind of retrieval means that new connections to other known words and their meanings are formed; this elaboration of existing knowledge contributes to learning and retention. Reading is an important retrieval activity of this type: it offers learners opportunities to encounter many previously met words in new contexts. Concordancing is an activity type that is intended to capture the experience of meeting a new word in a variety of reading contexts; a **concordance** is a list of examples of a word or phrase that are gathered from a corpus. Learners are asked to examine the concordance lines and draw conclusions. In Activity 2.1, the task is to determine the various possible meanings of *party*.

Activity 2.1

Imagine that a learner of English has previously met the word *party*, but does not yet know it well. The learner's task is to examine the concordance lines below and to think about the meaning of *party*. The concordance is drawn from a corpus of graded readers on the Lextutor website (see Lextutor concordancers in the Appendix).

a) We once met at a <u>party</u> where you had too much to drink and were very nice to me.
b) She had met him at a <u>party</u> in London, given by a Mrs Polswett.
c) He's expecting me to join a <u>party</u> on his yacht.
d) Pasha had never been a member of the Bolshevik <u>party</u>, and after the Civil War he was no longer considered a hero.
e) I can't let him organize a search <u>party</u>. I really can't.
f) Everybody thought it was right to wait for his return, and so the date of Simon's <u>party</u> was put off until Uncle Charles could be with them.
g) There was quite a little <u>party</u> to say goodbye to Flora at the station.
h) Analysts and <u>party</u> loyalists agree, it has a chance to reshape itself as the <u>party</u> of the center.
i) The whole <u>party</u> have left Netherfield, and are on their way back to London, probably for the winter.
j) The leader of the opposition Labor <u>party</u> today urged swift negotiations.
k) I'm giving a little supper <u>party</u> for some of the officers tomorrow.

1. If we assume the learner has partial knowledge of *party* as 'a social occasion to which people are invited to eat, drink, and enjoy themselves,' what new meaning associations might the learner make by examining the concordance lines?

2. On the basis of this activity, what assumption should the learner make about the most frequent meaning of *party*?

3. Research indicates that some words may be stored in the mental lexicon as core concepts; according to this view, access to a particular meaning sense is activated by the context of use. Is it possible to identify a core meaning that is shared across all the uses of *party*?

4. Look up the noun *party* in a dictionary. Does it show any meaning senses that are not exemplified in the concordance lines? Are there any other main entries for *party*?

5. How useful is this kind of activity in your view? Can you imagine doing concordancing activities with a group of learners you are familiar with? How might you adjust the activity for use with learners?

> 6 You can use the concordancer on the Lextutor website (see Appendix) to explore authentic uses of *party* or other words of your choice in a variety of English corpora. Use the menu to select a corpus. It is interesting to compare uses of a word in two corpora that can be expected to differ—spoken vs written, for example.

In teaching activities that foster elaboration, the focus is on enriching knowledge of words and building varied associations rather than on promoting ever more rapid retrieval of forms and meanings. Elaboration-focused teaching is referred to as **rich instruction** (Beck, McKeown, & Omanson, 1987). It typically involves integrating multiple aspects of word knowledge such as morphology, collocation, and grammatical features (Nation, 2008). For example, in working with the morphology of the word *portable*, the teacher can point out that the Latin root *port* means carry, ask students to think about other words they know that use this root (*transport, porter, export*, etc.), and discuss how the examples instantiate the *carry* concept. An elaborated treatment of *march* could draw attention to collocation by talking about the kinds of people who march (*soldiers, demonstrators, bands*), the words that can come after the verb (*into battle, through town, past*). The teacher can also build meaning associations by asking learners how marching differs from walking and running and encouraging them to talk about a time they saw people marching or marched in a parade themselves. They can even do some actual marching. Beck, McKeown, and Omanson (1987) emphasize the benefits of making such personalized experiential associations.

Writing and speaking activities can be designed to promote elaborative processing. For example, a task that requires learners to use new words in original sentences might push them to use different grammatical forms than occurred in the context where the word was first met. In a writing task, learners may need to use a verb in a different tense or change a verb to a noun. Using new words in writing stories or essays also involves connecting the new words to other words, ideas, and personal experiences in ways that differ from their use in the original encounter. Similarly, speaking or writing activities that ask learners to respond to a text they have read by giving their opinion on the content, retell the events from a different perspective, or devise a different ending to a story all involve using previously met words in new ways. Research by Joe (1998) confirms the word learning benefits of speaking activities that engage learners in elaborative processing.

The **keyword mnemonic** is a well-known and much studied example of an elaborative technique that makes use of imagery to link the meaning of a word to its spoken form. It involves thinking of an L1 word that sounds like the new L2 word and then creating a mental image that connects the L1 sound-alike to the meaning of the new L2 word. For example, a French-speaking learner of English meeting the word *flesh* might notice that it sounds like the French word *flèche* (arrow). Forming a mental image of flesh being pierced by an arrow would be helpful in connecting the sound of *flesh* to its meaning. The more improbable and vivid the image, the more memorable it is likely to be. Keywords need not be based on L1 words; familiar English words can also be used as mnemonics. For instance, teachers can point out that people who *falter* are often likely to *fall*; and the idea of thinking of *hugging* a big monster to remember the written form of *huge* was mentioned earlier in this chapter.

> **Activity 2.2**
> Keyword mnemonics can help make abstract, academic words memorable for young learners. Research points to high rates of retention for words learned using this method. Try to devise colorful keyword mnemonics for each of the following words, all taken from the MSVL (Greene & Coxhead, 2015).
> The following wording may be useful: New word X (or part of it) sounds like familiar word Y. Therefore, to remember X, I can think of [supply a mental image in which both X and Y are pictured].
>
> abandon
> category
> membrane
> document
> proceed
>
> 1 Can you imagine using this technique with a group of learners you are familiar with?
> 2 Who should make the keywords in your view? The teacher or the learners?

Skilled word learners initiate their own elaborations when they meet a new word. They may associate it with a personal experience, analyze the morphology, identify an L1 or L2 word with a similar meaning, look for a cognate connection across languages they know, note the collocating words that precede or follow the word, devise a keyword image, and more. But many learners need teaching that guides them in doing these useful kinds of thinking. When classroom vocabulary teaching includes elaboration, it has the potential to benefit learners in two important ways: it contributes to the learners' acquisition of new vocabulary through the development of rich networks of associative links to previous knowledge; it also provides learners with a model of how successful vocabulary learning happens. We will return to the second point in the discussion of sociocultural perspectives on vocabulary acquisition at the end of this chapter.

In the next section, we turn to the challenge of school reading, with special attention to the acquisition of academic vocabulary. We will also explore the **incidental learning hypothesis**, a research framework with particular relevance for learning vocabulary at school.

Vocabulary Acquisition at School

Children who first encounter English at school are often able to make rapid L2 word learning gains if they have well developed L1 vocabulary frameworks to build on. Their rates of acquisition may match or even outpace those of their English-speaking classmates (Paradis, 2007). But young native speakers have a substantial head start in the vocabulary learning process, and their vocabulary sizes are increasing, too. In trying to catch up, ELLs are trying to hit a moving target (Cummins, 2000). The vocabulary size shortfall persists and may even widen as ELLs move into high school. In Activity 2.3, you can explore vocabulary knowledge differences in samples of language produced by kindergarten-age ELLs and native speakers of English. The activity also gives a sense of the spoken vocabulary knowledge of children who have not yet been exposed to the vocabulary of academic reading at school.

> **Activity 2.3**
> You can compare the vocabulary used by young native speakers of English and ELLs using VocabProfile (VP-Kids) on the Lextutor website (see Appendix), which was introduced in Chapter 1. This tool analyzes the vocabulary of an entered text in terms of its use of words native English-speaking children know. The entered text is matched against ten 250-word frequency lists derived from speech productions by young English speakers (Stemach & Williams, 1988). The demos under the text entry box allow you to explore the vocabulary of a story about a boy, a dog, and a frog as told by young native speakers and ELLs.

1 To compare native and ELL vocabulary use in two children of the same age, begin by selecting the demo labeled 'NS2-5yr-1 mo' and clicking 'Submit'. (The label indicates that the child is a native speaker, aged five years and one month.) Note the distribution of the words across the frequency bands. Does this child use vocabulary from all ten bands? Also note the total proportion of very high-frequency words in Bands 1 and 2. The rightmost column of the output shows the cumulative percentages.

2 It is also interesting to scroll down to the see the 'off-list' words that appear in red. These are words not found in the VP-Kids frequency lists and are very rare or non-existent in English. How would you characterize the speaker's use of off-list words?

3 Next, select the story produced by an ELL of the same age labeled 'ELL-5yr-0mo' (indicating that the age of ELL speaker is five years and zero months) and compare. What do you notice about the distribution of words across the frequency bands? Also note the proportion of words from Bands 1 and 2. Is this child more or less reliant on high-frequency words than the native speaker? This child's use of an off-list word is also revealing.

4 Explore the other demos following the steps above or enter texts of your own. Be sure to remove the instructions from the window before pasting in your own text. Interesting texts to explore might be samples from children's literature or children's written productions.

Reading and the Vocabulary of School

In Chapter 1, we noted a turning point in the language of school at around fourth grade (Chall, 1996). In the earlier grades, the emphasis is on learning to read. Early reading instruction in English may focus on decoding skills with training that guides children in looking at letters and letter sequences on the page and sounding out the words. Other approaches to early reading emphasize the recognition of **sight words**, including frequently used words that are not easy to decode because of inconsistent letter–sound relationships; examples are *thought*, *know*, and *could* (Geva & Ramírez, 2015). The materials used to teach reading are simple story texts that feature familiar spoken language like, 'Look, Brad! There's a big brown bear!' But from Grade 4 onwards, the emphasis shifts to reading to learn new information from expository texts. Children are expected to be able to read sentences like 'Brown bears are found in the coastal areas of British Columbia and Alaska', not just as reading practice but for the purpose of understanding new information and working with it. For example, a classroom task might ask them to use the information to color in bear habitats on a map. This requires the ability to locate British Columbia and Alaska on a map as well as a clear understanding of the words *coastal* and *area*, words that may not be very familiar to fourth graders. Corpus searches indicate that both words occur much more frequently in writing than in speech; VP-Kids analysis shows that neither is found on the Kid Talk lists of the 2,500 most frequent word families in oral productions produced by young L1 English speakers (Stemach & Williams, 1988).

Corpus research shows that everyday spoken language and 'school' language in the written mode differ greatly in terms of vocabulary. Corson's (1995) exploration of the two modes found that words used frequently in conversations tend to be short and Anglo-Saxon in origin, while words used in academic writing are longer and largely borrowed from Latin and Greek—with little overlap between the two. *Definition, perspective,* and *attribute* are examples of Greco-Latin words. Like many academic words, their meanings are rather abstract; they are unlikely to be heard on the playground. Acquiring the Greco-Latin vocabulary that is typically used to explain concepts in school texts from Grade 4 onwards resembles learning a new language, and it presents challenges for native English speakers and ELLs alike.

Cummins (2008) found that high levels of conversational fluency in English, which he terms **basic interpersonal communicative skills** (**BICS**) are relatively easy for children to acquire. Most native speakers have these skills by age six and ELLs can acquire them in two years of exposure to the new language (Cummins, 2008). But good conversation skills can be misleading if educators assume they indicate high levels of ability to use the language of school, which Cummins refers to as **cognitive academic language proficiency** (**CALP**). He found that ELLs needed five to seven years of exposure to English at school to master CALP. As Heibert (2012) points out, the learning task is not simple. A critical part of CALP is academic vocabulary, and knowledge of this vocabulary entails recognizing the derived and inflected forms of root words and multiple meanings such words can have. Corson (1995) sees failure to acquire the Greco-Latin vocabulary of academic English as a 'lexical bar'; those who do not master it are denied access to the world of educational opportunity.

In Chapter 1, we introduced the Academic Word List (AWL) and Middle School Vocabulary Lists (MSVL). These lists were made with the express purpose of identifying the words of this 'foreign' vocabulary that is needed for school. Other well-known efforts to identify the vocabulary of school include work on core vocabulary (Zeno, Ivens, Millard, & Duvvuri, 1995) and Tier 2 words (Beck et al., 1987).

The divide between the vocabulary of spoken English and academic writing contributes to what Chall and Jacobs (2003) have termed the 'grade four slump' in reading ability, a problem that is especially pronounced in children from less advantaged families. The implications for further vocabulary development are profound. Although some new words can be taught in school and new vocabulary continues to be acquired through exposure to spoken language, reading is recognized as the main source of new vocabulary knowledge in the school-age years and onwards into adulthood (Nagy, Herman, & Anderson, 1985).

Reading is so important because written language is where new words are most likely to be found. Written language needs to be lexically rich in order to describe things the reader cannot see. In speech, by contrast, the real world context around the speaker often helps make the meaning clear. We can see this in the bear example given earlier in this chapter (see page 55). There is no need for the speaker to use vocabulary typical of the written mode to explain to Brad that the *position* of the bear is *adjacent* to the *vehicle* because they can both see the bear in front of them. The natural lexical poverty of ordinary speech is an argument for reading stories aloud to preschool children; the written language of stories exposes children to a richer vocabulary than they are likely to hear in conversations (Cunningham, 2005; Nation, 2006).

Activity 2.4

To explore the vocabulary differences between first and fourth grade school materials, compare the following texts using the VP-Kids tool (described in Activity 2.3). Make and save versions of the samples; you need not type the punctuation. Analyze each text separately.

To what extent does each consist of high-frequency words that children are likely to know? To assess this, compare the proportions accounted for by frequency Bands 1 and 2 in each. Also scroll down to see the words and their distribution over the frequency bands. Do the Grade 4 words in the 'off-list but known word' category have an academic flavor in your view?

Grade 1

'I wish I had a fish to eat,' said Max. 'Then we will catch a big fish,' said Grandma. 'We can walk to the park,' said Ruby. 'And Max will catch a big fish.' 'Good,' said Max. 'Yum, yum, yum!' The path in the park led to the pond. 'Max can fish in this pond,' said Ruby. Max sat. He got a red ball in his net. But no fish bit.

(Scott-Foresman Reading Street)

Grade 4

There are four separate stages in the life of a butterfly: The egg is a tiny, round or oval shape that gets attached by the female butterfly to a leaf, stem or other object. The egg is usually attached near the intended caterpillar food. The caterpillar or larva is the long, worm-like state of the butterfly. It sometimes has an interesting pattern of stripes or patches.

(Sample worksheet from www.k5learning.com)

Try investigating other text samples using VP-Kids. If you have access to early primary reading materials and textbooks used in Grade 4 or later, analyze samples from these and compare the results. Samples should be at least 50 words long for valid comparisons. Do your findings confirm the idea that learning to read texts differ from reading to learn texts in terms of their vocabulary?

Incidental Vocabulary Learning

The idea that reading is good for building new vocabulary is widely accepted. We assume that when readers meet unfamiliar words in their reading, they use their understanding of the text to work out the meanings of some of these words. Even though they are likely to be focused on understanding the message of the text rather than individual words, we can expect that they will hold at least a few of the new form–meaning connections in memory. Gaining new word knowledge in this manner is referred to as **incidental vocabulary learning**. Hulstijn (2001) defines incidental vocabulary acquisition as the 'learning of vocabulary as the by-product of any activity not explicitly geared to vocabulary learning' (2001, p. 271). It stands in contrast to **intentional vocabulary learning** where the learner makes a deliberate effort to commit new words to memory. Vocabulary acquisition in early childhood is incidental in character. As children attend to the spoken language around them, they are hardly making mental lists of new words to study and remember. Any new words they pick up incidentally while trying to understand the language around them can be seen as a (useful) by-product of the comprehension process.

Investigations of incidental vocabulary acquisition are important because they help delineate the teacher's role. If learners could easily acquire all the word knowledge they need 'for free' through incidental processes, there would be no reason to spend valuable class time on teaching vocabulary! The question of academic vocabulary is particularly critical to consider here. Can learners acquire it incidentally on their own or is there a need for instruction and intentional learning?

Incidental Acquisition Through Reading

The idea that a great deal of vocabulary knowledge is acquired through reading has been put forward as the incidental learning hypothesis (Nagy et al., 1985). According to this hypothesis, 'incidental learning from context during free reading is the major mode of vocabulary acquisition during the school years' (p. 234). The proponents of the hypothesis argue that the thousands of words that adult native speakers eventually come to know could not possibly all have been taught and learned at school; therefore, people must be picking up new word knowledge from their reading. We have seen that academic vocabulary is not likely to be heard to any great extent in everyday conversations; this suggests that school reading is likely to be an important resource for learning academic words.

There is ample research evidence to support the idea that people acquire new vocabulary knowledge through reading. In their investigation of primary and middle school children who read short age-appropriate school texts, Nagy et al. (1985) found that they gained new word knowledge at the average rate of about 1 in 10. That is, of 10 unfamiliar words met in context while reading, 1 was remembered well enough for the reader to be able to identify a correct definition on a surprise multiple-choice test administered after the reading of the passages. This may not seem like an impressive rate, but taken over many years of reading, it can account for a great deal of vocabulary growth. Many investigations of L2 readers confirm that they also learn new words through reading; but as with L1 readers, the growth rates are small. Many studies report gains of just one or two words as the result of reading a short passage (Horst, Cobb, & Meara, 1998). Zahar, Cobb, and Spada's (2001) investigation of seventh-grade ESL learners showed that they acquired knowledge of new words met in a graded reader at the rate of 1 in 14. There is no doubt that incidental vocabulary acquisition is real, but we are left with the question of whether the process is powerful enough to do the job of helping L2 learners acquire substantial numbers of academic words during their years at school. Research discussed in the next section delineates the scope of the learning task and addresses this question.

Comprehensibility and Volume

For learners to be able to acquire knowledge of new words through reading, the materials they read must contain some words that they do not already know. At the same time, texts need to be understood well enough for readers to be able to infer the meanings of the unknown words that are found in them. It is worth noting that successful guessing of a new word's meaning from context does not guarantee that the new form–meaning connection will be remembered, but it is obviously an essential first step in the incidental learning process. Learning from this type of reading material echoes theoretical work by Krashen (1982), who proposed that access to **comprehensible input** is a crucial condition for L2 acquisition. In his work, the comprehensible input that promotes learning is described somewhat elusively as language that is one step beyond the learner's current stage of linguistic competence.

A more specific answer to the question of what makes reading material 'just right' in terms of both comprehensibility and opportunities for learning new words comes from research that has investigated L2 reading comprehension in relation to proportions of known and unknown words in texts. As might be expected, higher levels of known words lead to higher levels of comprehension. An investigation of university learners of English by Schmitt, Jiang, and Grabe (2011) showed that when 98% of the words are familiar—amounting to just one unfamiliar word in 50—the chances that L2 readers will be able to read the text independently and understand it adequately are good. Hiebert (2012) recommends a similar 98–99% coverage criterion for primary-school L1 readers and suggests that knowledge of 4,000 basic families is useful in reaching a high level of coverage of school readings. Greene's (2008) analysis of an eighth-grade science textbook indicated that middle school students would need to know the 7,000 most frequent English word families to recognize 95% of the words in the text. Nation's (2006) study of reading materials intended for adults determined that knowledge of 8,000 to 9,000 word families is needed to achieve the recommended 98% coverage level. In his calculations, it is assumed that the reader will also know all the proper nouns that occur in a text. While the findings vary, all of them indicate that the number of word families readers need to know in order to comprehend school materials is very large.

Because readers pick up knowledge of only a few of the new words they meet in their reading, they need to read a great deal in order for any significant amount of new vocabulary learning to occur. Nagy et al. (1985) estimated that school age learners typically read over one million words per year in their L1—the equivalent of roughly ten adult-size novels—and concluded that this amount of reading accounts for gains of about 1,000 new words per year during the school years. However, this is probably an optimistic scenario; in a study of fifth graders in an American school, estimates based on logs of time spent reading indicated that readers in the middle range read around 300,000 words per year (Anderson, Wilson, & Fielding, 1988). It is safe to say many school-aged L2 readers will have difficulty achieving the goal of reading hundreds of thousands of words per year, and that a million words is probably well beyond the reach of most.

Readers need to process a large amount of text for another reason: words need to be encountered repeatedly in order for them to stay in memory. This means reading in enough volume to meet new words and to retrieve their meanings many times. Multiple encounters are also important because retrievals in varying contexts help learners delineate the possible meanings a word can have and its uses. Studies of incidental vocabulary acquisition suggest that as many as ten encounters are needed for a new form–meaning connection to be retained (Nation, 2013). Zahar, Cobb, and Spada's (2001) investigation of seventh grade ESL learners showed that multiple encounters are particularly important for less proficient learners. In a study of university L2 learners, Horst, Cobb, and Meara (1998) found that most of the words met eight times or more in a graded ESL reader were identified correctly on a test given after the reading was completed. Frequent words at the 1,000 and 2,000 levels were recycled many times in the book; however, only six words that were not high-frequency and likely to be unfamiliar to the low-intermediate students were repeated eight times or more in the 21,000-word story.

This minimal recycling of all but the most frequent words is a natural characteristic of texts (Zipf, 1935, 1949). That is, patterning following **Zipf's law** indicates that as learners come to know more words and the chances of meeting unfamiliar words decrease, the chances of meeting new words repeatedly diminish exponentially (Nation, 2013). A study by Cobb (2007) further illustrates the problem. His analyses showed that in reading a million words of materials designed for native speakers, readers would encounter 1,000- and 2,000-level words repeatedly, but fewer than half of the words on the 3,000-level list would be encountered six times or more; and only a small fraction of 4,000-level words met this criterion. Overcoming this obstacle to incidental acquisition clearly requires a very large volume of reading, and we can conclude that the conditions for learning large numbers of new mid-frequency and academic words simply through reading place unrealistically high demands on L2 learners.

For those who can easily accomplish a great deal of reading, the vocabulary benefits accumulate in a 'rich get richer' scenario. The more they read, the more opportunities they have to encounter new words and learn them, and the easier it becomes to read more challenging materials. Meanwhile, their classmates who struggle with reading make their way through far less text with fewer opportunities to encounter and learn the new words that would make their reading easier. Thus, the gap in vocabulary that many less advantaged L1 and L2 learners start out with in the early grades becomes ever wider over their years at school (Stanovich, 1986). These realities constitute an argument for explicit classroom instruction that systematically targets large numbers of the words learners need to know. In Chapters 3 and 4, we will take a close look at ambitious programs of rich instruction that set out to bridge the gap by targeting academic vocabulary.

Supporting Word Learning Through Reading

The finding that a level of known-word coverage on the order of 98% is needed to support reading comprehension has a clear message for teachers. Too often, young L1 and L2 readers are confronted with texts that contain too many unknown words, resulting in frustration and incomprehension. Reading school textbooks that are increasingly loaded with academic vocabulary after third grade is particularly problematic (Hiebert, 2012). A way of easing the transition into this type of reading is to create materials that gradually introduce small numbers of academic words in easy contexts and recycle the new words often. Graded readers for learners of English are designed for easy comprehensibility and are useful for the acquisition of high-frequency words. As L2 learners become more proficient readers, they can read literature written for child and adolescent L1 readers, but a caveat is in order: they should be strongly encouraged to read some non-fiction titles. Though many young learners may find fiction more motivating to read, it features far fewer of the academic words that school readers most need to know (Gardner, 2004, 2008).

Drawing learners' attention to academic vocabulary and other useful words as they occur in classroom reading (and listening) passages can help accelerate the slow pace of incidental vocabulary learning. Investigations of the design of reading activities show that vocabulary exercises that engage learners in working with some of the words in a reading passage lead to stronger vocabulary gains than requiring the learners to simply read the passage and answer comprehension questions (Hulstijn & Laufer, 2001; Paribakht & Wesche, 1996). Activities that involve learners in rereading and retelling a passage are effective ways of creating opportunities for retrieval of partially known words. Learners are engaged in using the new words productively in a meaningful context (Nation, 2008).

Instructors can also teach strategies for making new words that are met in texts easier to understand and remember. These include raising learners' awareness of helpful L1 cognates, showing them how to exploit word-part knowledge, and developing contextual guessing skills. We will return to these strategies in Chapters 3 and 4. Teachers can also show students what elaborative word processing is like by thinking aloud with them about the words they meet in classroom readings. This idea is explored further in the discussion of sociocultural theory at the end of this chapter.

Finally, even though learners may not gain full knowledge of the meanings of large numbers of new words from a reading experience, there are other good reasons to encourage them to read. Reading offers important opportunities to notice words and acquire partial knowledge. Eye-tracking studies confirm that learners notice new words in their reading even if the word is encountered only once (Godfroid, Housen, & Boers, 2010). Case studies using sensitive measures have identified small gains in partial knowledge of L2 word meanings over the course of meeting new words repeatedly (Horst & Meara, 1999). In addition to knowledge of word meanings, learners gain awareness of the grammatical functions, associations, and collocations of words (Pigada & Schmitt, 2006; Webb, 2007). Meeting familiar words repeatedly in texts is also important for the development of fluency (Nation, 2008).

Word Learning Through Viewing

In their 1985 publication, Nagy, Herman, and Anderson focused on incidental learning of vocabulary through reading, but the potential to learn vocabulary through exposure to other kinds of input should not be overlooked. There is research evidence that extra-curricular activities such as watching film and television is beneficial for vocabulary acquisition—more so than many educators and parents might expect. Investigations of film and television corpora show that, while these media tend to recycle many frequent words that are likely to be familiar, a typical film or television program also provides opportunities for exposure to infrequent words that are less likely to be known (Rodgers & Webb, 2011; Webb & Rodgers, 2009). Since most people watch much more television than they read, the potential for learning new L2 vocabulary through viewing is considerable (Peters & Webb, 2018; Webb & Nation, 2017). Neuman and Koskinen (1992) found that middle school ELLs acquired more new vocabulary by watching a video than through reading; the availability of visual support for new words seems a likely explanation. Studies have also examined other media besides film and television. Sylvén and Sundqvist (2012) showed that Swedish teenagers acquire English vocabulary incidentally through playing computer games. Cobb and Horst (2011) found that amounts of time spent playing word games on a handheld device were associated with gains in middle school ESL learners' receptive and productive vocabulary size and speed of lexical access. What all of these studies tell us is that more research is needed to clarify incidental vocabulary learning processes in a digital world where L1 and L2 learners interact with spoken and written English in new ways—in and out of class.

In this discussion of incidental vocabulary acquisition, we have explored the potential and limitations of learning vocabulary through exposure to input. In the next section, we explore a theoretical perspective that emphasizes the importance of bringing teachers and learners together in conversations about the input and the vocabulary found in it.

The Sociocultural Perspective

The concepts underlying the sociocultural approach have evolved from work by psychologist Lev Vygotsky, who studied children's interactions and their conversations with adults. Vygotsky (1978) concluded that language and cognition develop largely through social interaction. Thinking and speaking go hand in hand, and learners can reach higher levels of cognitive development by participating in conversations that support, stretch, and build on the knowledge they already have. Classroom Snapshot 2.2 illustrates how a teacher who is interested in implementing the sociocultural approach applies these ideas in reading a story with learners. She elaborates on words by sharing the personal associations the words evoke for her and expresses her thoughts in accessible and conversational language, inviting her students to do this kind of thinking for themselves.

Classroom Snapshot 2.2

Here is an example of how Jan Wells, a teacher of fourth- and fifth-grade learners (L1 English and ELLs) in Canada, thinks aloud with her students while reading to them. She asks the students to raise their hands when they hear any vocabulary they find striking. These are noted as 'Gifts of Words' and entered into the class 'Bank of Powerful Language', which is used as a resource in writing projects later.

Teacher: I'm going to read aloud from a book with very special language. It's a lovely story about a boy waking up and hearing all sorts of sounds. Just listen to how the author helps us to hear the sounds the boy hears.

Teacher: [reading aloud] 'Beyond the rim of morning the sun ticks, the birds talk and the spoons sleep nestled in the kitchen drawers. First light melts like butter on pancakes, spreads warm and yellow across your pillow.'

Teacher: When I hear the words 'the sun ticks,' I think of a clock ticking. I think about how the sun is like a clock, moving across the sky as the day passes. When the day is over, night falls, and it gets dark. So the author thinks of the sun like a clock telling us that time is passing during the day.

Teacher: [reading aloud again] 'After supper the night creeps in and the moon spills milk for the cat to drink.'

Teacher: When I read this, I think about a pool of spilled milk, all white and glistening. The author makes me think that the moonlight must be very bright and that it looks like a puddle of milk on the floor. It paints a really vivid picture in my mind. Listen to some more of the story and let's see if there are any more examples of this powerful language. I'll read really slowly, and you can put up your hand if you hear a Gift of Words.

(Scott, Skobell, & Wells, 2016: 46)

Scott, Skobell, and Wells (2016) advocate a Vygotskyan approach to teaching vocabulary in primary schools with diverse learner populations that include ELLs. They emphasize the importance of classroom interactions that raise 'word consciousness' and invite young learners to join and participate in a word-learning community. This is especially important for learning academic vocabulary, which children encounter in a kind of discourse that is unfamiliar to many of them. Teachers are encouraged to help learners see academic vocabulary as a powerful tool they can employ in expressing ideas precisely, a useful kind of language they can add to their existing linguistic repertoires. Implementing the approach requires sensitivity and skill; in attempting to build on their students' home language and literacy practices, teachers must sometimes reach across wide cultural and linguistic divides (Scott, Nagy, & Flinsbach, 2008). The effects of training designed to develop teachers' word consciousness were investigated in a study by Scott, Miller, and Flinsbach (2012). Results showed that the training raised the teachers' awareness of vocabulary and impacted their teaching. Children in the word-conscious classrooms learned more vocabulary than children in comparable classrooms taught by teachers who had not participated in the training.

By sharing their personal associations with words and communicating enthusiasm for learning new vocabulary, teachers model a way of thinking that may be contagious. With so many words to know and not enough time to study them all in class, discovering how to become an effective independent vocabulary learner may be one of the most important lessons students learn at school.

Summary

This chapter explored theories and research that address the question of how the human mind learns words. A consistent theme was the role of exposure to language input. Children attend to the world around them and the input they hear to develop form–meaning connections and make links between words used together frequently in the input. Eventually, a complex network of linked words, phrases, and meanings evolves. We saw that when input is limited, children's vocabulary development suffers. On a more positive note, we saw that when their L1 vocabulary knowledge is well developed, this supports the acquisition of vocabulary in the L2. Another theme we discussed was cognitive processing capacity. The mental system is easily overwhelmed and, when a new word is first met in a stream of language input, there may only be enough spare capacity available to notice it and perhaps attend to a single aspect such as its form. Over the course of multiple retrievals, form–meaning connections can become automatized, leaving more cognitive resources available for other tasks. For instance, mental resources can be devoted to guessing the meanings of new words in the input and associating them with other words and other kinds of knowledge and experience. Engaging in such 'costly' elaborative processing has been shown to be a highly worthwhile learning investment.

In the discussion of investigations of the incidental learning hypothesis, we saw that the vocabulary demands of school reading are very high; in order to comprehend school texts, learners need to know thousands of high- and mid-frequency word families and hundreds of academic families. One approach to tackling this very large task is instruction that involves students in the deliberate study of words. Theory and research offer guidelines for designing learning activities that are effective and efficient. It is also important to show students how to become effective autonomous vocabulary learners. Training in strategies for determining the meanings of new words and modelling word consciousness were discussed in this chapter as ways of making reading a more powerful resource for learning new vocabulary independently. In Chapters 3 and 4, we will discover how these ideas have been implemented in the real world of classroom learning.

3
Vocabulary Acquisition in Young Learners of English

Preview
This chapter describes how primary school ELLs develop their vocabulary knowledge. We will look at the vocabulary growth of young learners in different educational contexts and consider factors that can support or hinder their development. We also examine the various ways in which their knowledge of English vocabulary develops. The final sections of the chapter focus on vocabulary instruction that has proven to be effective in supporting young learners' achievement at school.

English Vocabulary Growth in Primary School
In 1984, Saville-Troike published a study with the provocative title 'What really matters in second language learning for academic achievement?' This investigation of primary ELLs awakened many educators and researchers to the importance of vocabulary, and the themes of this seminal study continue to resonate today.

Spotlight Study 3.1
The children Saville-Troike investigated knew no or very little English at the beginning of the school year. They were placed in mainstream classes for L1 English speakers in a public school, in a university community in the United States, and given support for their language development in the form of pull-out ESL classes. The children ranged in age from 7 to 12 years. They were advantaged in that they came from well-educated, middle-class families; all had at least one parent with a graduate-level university degree. Because the children would be returning to schooling in their home countries at the end of the year, most were also taught in their L1 (Japanese, Korean, Hebrew, and Arabic) for 30 minutes every day.

The researcher and her team expected the school experience of these advantaged children to be a great success story. They explored a host of variables including the learners' knowledge of English syntax and morphology, their oral proficiency in English, attitudes to learning, levels of social interaction in English as observed on the playground, **communicative competence** as observed in videotaped ESL classes, home language use, literacy practices at home, personality factors, and more. The goal of the research was to determine which of these factors were most closely associated with success in learning school subjects. At the end of the school year, the learners took a standardized test designed for L1 English-speaking students with subtests for reading, mathematics, science, and other school subjects.

Contrary to expectation, performance on the end-of-year school tests did not tell a story of unmitigated success. Scores ranged widely, with astonishing progress for some and virtually no academic achievement at all for others. For example, after just one year of schooling in English, one exceptional Japanese third-grader scored in the 65th percentile on the test of English reading and in the 99th percentile on the test of English language skills. Interviews with her parents and teachers revealed that she read several years above her grade level in Japanese, and was considered to have unusually high levels of Japanese vocabulary and grammar knowledge for a child her age.

What makes this study particularly important is the finding that, of the many factors investigated, only one—productive English vocabulary size—was strongly associated with performance on the school tests. Vocabulary size was measured in terms of the number of different words the child produced in an extensive oral interview that involved telling a favorite folktale. The author concludes unequivocally that 'vocabulary knowledge is the single most important area of second language (L2) competence when learning content through that language' (Saville-Troike, 1984, p. 199). Based on this conclusion, she recommends that ESL instructors focus on teaching vocabulary that is closely related to the subject matter taught in mainstream classes.

Somewhat surprisingly, other language-related variables such as grammatical accuracy and communicative competence proved to have little relation to the ELLs' academic achievement. Given this result, the author questions whether time spent on teaching grammar in ESL lessons is a good investment for learners at this early phase of L2 acquisition. Since this study appeared, many other studies have confirmed the association between vocabulary knowledge and performance at school; recent research points to the value of focusing teaching on academic vocabulary. Many of the issues raised in Saville-Troike's (1984) study continue to be relevant. Among topics that we will return to in this chapter are the effects of bilingual instruction, parents' level of education, and L1 literacy.

Many researchers have investigated the vocabulary learning trajectory of learners of English in primary schools. Questions addressed in the next section include: How quickly can young ELLs learn English vocabulary at school? Can they ever catch up with their native English-speaking classmates whose vocabulary is also growing?

How Much? How Fast?

Primary school children know thousands of words. According to research by Biemiller and Slonim (2001), L1 English-speaking children in American schools know over 5,000 word families by the end of second grade. How many do they learn in a year? A study that looked at varying levels of performance on a vocabulary size test indicated that L1 English-speaking learners at the average level acquired around 840 families per year in primary school (Biemiller & Boote, 2006). In the below-average group, which included some ELLs, gains were substantially lower at 570 families per year. However, as we will see, other studies show that many ELLs can make sizable gains at a pace that matches or exceeds that of their L1 English-speaking classmates.

A measure that is often used to track vocabulary development in both learners and native speakers of English is the Peabody Picture Vocabulary Test (PPVT). It was originally developed in 1959 by education specialists Lloyd and Leota Dunn, and is designed for testing knowledge of Standard American English. The PPVT has been revised several times, most recently in 2007. Adjustments have been made to reduce the race, ethnic, and gender biases of the original images and versions have been created for other languages. The current version (PPVT-R) consists of a series of 228 pages with four pictures on each page. For example, a page presents pictures of a mother holding a baby, a girl laughing, a boy sleeping, and a man walking a dog. The examiner says to the child, 'Put your finger on *laughing*'. The tested words are progressively more difficult, and the testing stops when the child makes eight or more errors in a set of 12. The test is a measure of receptive vocabulary knowledge; that is, it assesses the child's ability to recognize a pictured meaning in response to a spoken form. Researchers also use picture-naming tasks to assess productive vocabulary. Because the PPVT does not require reading, it can be given to children as young as two and a half years old. Thousands of children and adults in the United States and Canada have taken the test, and its age and grade norms are well established.

The PPVT does not provide estimates of a test taker's overall English vocabulary size; instead, the child's performance is related to the performance of other test takers of the same age. A new computerized test, the Picture Vocabulary Size Test (PVST) has been developed by Anthony and Nation (2017) to address the need for a size test suitable for use with children and preliterate learners of English. The test words on the PVST are taken from lists of the 6,000 most frequently occurring word families in a 5-million-word corpus consisting of materials for young readers and spoken language taken from American and British sources. The child clicks on one of four pictures in response to hearing an audio cue such as 'It's a calf'. Each of the 96 test words represents 62.5 word families in the source lists. Thus, a child's vocabulary size can be determined by multiplying the number of correct responses by 62.5. For example, a child with a score of 70 has an approximate receptive vocabulary size of 4,375 word families. The PVST is available on Laurence Anthony's website (see Appendix). In Chapter 4, we will explore corpus-based size testing in more detail and you will have an opportunity to test your own English vocabulary size.

The PPVT and its Spanish counterpart, *Test de Vocabulario en Imagenes Peabody* (TVIP), were used in a study of language dominance in young bilinguals in the United States. The question of interest was the amount of exposure needed for the learners' knowledge of English vocabulary to overtake their Spanish vocabulary knowledge. The researchers investigated children from Spanish-speaking families who had first encountered English in school programs in the United States at the age of five (Kohnert & Bates, 2002). Scores on the Spanish and English tests of receptive vocabulary knowledge were roughly equal in learners aged 11 years or younger, but test-takers older than 11 performed better on the English measure. In other words, six years of exposure to English represented a turning point; those who were over 11 had become English dominant, at least with regard to receptive vocabulary knowledge.

Because the PPVT interprets scores in terms of age norms that have been established previously by administering the test to thousands of L1 English speakers, it is possible to administer the PPVT to an ELL, check the score against the age norms, and arrive at the child's 'vocabulary age' for English. In an interesting case study using this methodology, Winitz, Gillespie, and Starcev (1995) investigated an eight-year-old Polish-speaking immigrant with little previous knowledge of English. He was placed in a rural school in Missouri where there was no ESL support. According to PPVT results, his English vocabulary knowledge at the outset of the study was just under the norm for two-year-old L1 English speakers. But when he was tested again after one year of exposure to English at school, his vocabulary age was just under the norm for six-year-olds. This remarkable child had advanced four years in terms of English vocabulary in only 12 months.

A study using a similar methodology tracked ELLs who were exposed to English in kindergarten and early primary school in Canada over a period of almost three years (Goldberg, Paradis, Crago, 2008). A few of the learners made large gains in a short period like the Polish boy described above, but they were exceptions. Overall, the testing showed that the immigrant children increased their English vocabulary knowledge such that by the end of the three years, their performance on the PPVT was close to the L1 norm for children of their age. This is a more positive outcome than has been reported in other studies. In another Canadian study, learners in mainstream classrooms who were regularly taken out to receive English language support were tracked over a six-year period from Grade 1 to Grade 6. The young ELLs developed their English vocabulary at a faster rate than their L1 English-speaking classmates, but even after six years, they had not caught up to native speakers of the same age (Farnia & Geva, 2011).

Indeed, most studies that use the PPVT to assess the English vocabulary development of primary ELLs identify a lag in comparison to the age norms for L1 English for native speakers (Uchikoshi, 2014). We saw this in the study of young Spanish–English bilinguals in Spotlight Study 2.1 (see page 38). Other studies using different kinds of vocabulary tests also confirm the lag (August, Carlo, Dressler, & Snow, 2005). We can conclude that although primary ELLs can achieve a great deal of English vocabulary growth at school, often at an accelerated pace, most will not manage to catch up with their L1 English classmates. Vocabulary instruction designed to address the shortfall is described later in this chapter.

Explanations for Growth

In the previous section, we saw that L2 vocabulary size gains are variable. Some studies reported much stronger vocabulary learning results than others; some exceptional learners were able to make very rapid progress. In this section, we look more closely at explanations for different learning outcomes. First, we consider factors in the circumstances surrounding the learner.

Amount of Exposure

An important factor that is associated with the rate of growth and eventual vocabulary size is amount of exposure to English input. More exposure means more opportunities for learning new words incidentally through hearing and reading language in use, and more scope for consolidating partially acquired vocabulary. It may also mean more intentional vocabulary learning in ESL support programs or content classes at school. There is strong research evidence for the connection between greater amounts of exposure and higher scores on the PPVT or other vocabulary measures (Goldberg, Paradis, & Crago, 2008; Milton & Meara, 1995).

Amount of exposure to English is often measured in terms of the numbers of months or years young ELLs spend in school. But, as might be expected, exposure to English at home can also benefit L2 vocabulary acquisition (Cobo-Lewis, Pearson, Eilers, & Umbel, 2002). Exposure to English outside home and school is more available in some linguistic communities than in others. Goldberg, Paradis, and Crago (2008) suggest that the relatively rapid growth trajectory of the ELLs they investigated in western Canada may be explained by the greater opportunities to practice English outside of the classroom than may be available to learners in places like Miami, Florida, where children live in a large Spanish-speaking community.

There is no single answer to the question of how much exposure it takes for young L2 learners to attain the English vocabulary knowledge they need. Research by Cummins (2008; discussed in Chapter 2) indicates that as many as five to seven years of exposure to English at school are required if acquiring CALP is the goal. Vocabulary studies discussed in the previous section suggest that, apart from a few cases of exceptional learners, at least several years of exposure at school are needed to achieve gains that are substantial. And though gains may be impressive, the gap between ELLs and their L1 English-speaking peers usually remains. Thousands of hours of continued exposure to English input over six years of primary school were not enough for ELLs to catch up with their classmates in the research reported by Farnia and Geva (2011). It is worth noting, however, that the vocabulary size differences between the two groups diminished with continued exposure as the children grew older.

In their longitudinal study, Farnia and Geva (2011) also showed that the ELLs' vocabulary growth was particularly rapid in the lower grades and then tapered off from Grade 3 onward. The likely explanation for initial rapid growth is the availability of many unfamiliar words to learn. In other words, the exposure factor may be at its most powerful in the beginning stages of vocabulary development because there is so much room to grow and many of the words that young L2 learners need to learn are the high-frequency words that occur in a variety of situations. As learning proceeds and many of these frequent words become known, the chances of repeated exposure to new and unfamiliar words diminishes.

Content and Language Integrated Learning (CLIL) programs in Europe and elsewhere are expressly designed to offer young majority-language students the benefits of increased exposure to L2 input. In a study of the effects of added exposure, Agustín-Llach and Canga Alonso (2014) compared the vocabulary development of fourth, fifth, and sixth-grade learners of English in CLIL programs and regular EFL classes in Spain. In addition to their regular EFL classes, the CLIL students had 300 hours of exposure to the L2 in science classes that were taught in English. Testing revealed that students in both the CLIL and regular groups learned many high-frequency English word families, but no substantial vocabulary size differences between learners in the two programs of study were found. It appears that the 300 additional hours were not enough for the exposure factor to have an effect. This study adds to the evidence that very large amounts of exposure—thousands rather than hundreds of hours—are needed to make a sizable impact on the L2 vocabulary growth of young learners.

Home and Family

Socioeconomic status (SES) is another influential factor. Studies of both L1 and L2 vocabulary development show that growth is faster in children who come from more advantaged families (Goldberg, Paradis, & Crago, 2008). Spotlight Study 2.2 (see page 43) is a famous example of research that has revealed dramatic differences between the L1 vocabulary sizes of children from advantaged and less advantaged families (Hart & Risley, 2003).

In investigations of English vocabulary learning, researchers often measure SES in terms of the mother's level of education in years. A study of young ELLs in Canada using this measure found SES to be the strongest predictor of L2 vocabulary development of the variables they investigated (Goldberg, Paradis, & Crago, 2008). Similarly, a study of L1 Spanish ELLs conducted in Miami found that the learners whose performance on a measure of vocabulary knowledge most closely matched L1 norms were children from high-SES families (Cobo-Lewis et al., 2002).

What accounts for the vocabulary advantage of children from high-SES families? As we saw in Spotlight Study 2.2, higher SES levels tend to go hand in hand with greater quantities of speech addressed to children in the home. There is also evidence that the quality of speech is more richly varied in these advantaged homes. Hart and Risley (2003) found that children in the high-SES homes they investigated heard almost 400 different words per hour in the parent talk they were exposed to, while children in the less advantaged homes heard well under half this number. In their investigation of Canadian ELLs, Goldberg, Paradis, and Crago (2008) found that mothers with higher levels of education used a greater variety of English words.

We might assume that in families with higher levels of maternal education, minority-language children have more exposure to English; well-educated parents might seem more likely to know and use English in the home than less well-educated ones. But research does not support this assumption. In the Miami study by Cobo-Lewis, Pearson, Eilers, and Umbel (2002), high-SES levels did not always go hand in hand with amounts of exposure to English in the family; many of the mothers in high-SES families told the researchers that even though they knew English well, they preferred to use Spanish in the home. In the Canadian research by Goldberg, Paradis, and Crago (2008), the children with more highly educated mothers tended to be those who were actually getting less exposure to English at home. This has led researchers to speculate that the quality of input in the home may be more important for L2 vocabulary development than the specific language used to deliver it. Activity 3.1 explores this possibility.

Activity 3.1

Spotlight Study 2.2 outlined 'The Early Catastrophe' for low-SES learners in terms of the quantity of parental input to which they were exposed. The authors of this study also investigated the quality of the input and identified a negative tone and a scarcity of child-affirming language in speech addressed to children in poor families. Five recommendations for caregivers based on their work have been summarized by Roberts (2009, p. 75) as follows:

- Just talk (many words, and many kinds of words).
- Be nice when talking (affirm rather than prohibit or criticize).
- Tell children about things in the home and community.
- Give children choices in talking.
- Listen to what children say, and show this by responding to them.

1. Imagine implementing the five recommendations with a child who does not know much English. How might each work to facilitate vocabulary learning?
2. Reflect on the quality of the input you heard at home in your childhood or the language addressed to children in families that you know. To what extent were/are these recommendations followed?
3. Why might it be difficult for low-SES parents to implement these recommendations?

4 Some have argued strenuously that Hart and Risley's work pathologizes the poor and is racially biased (Dudley-Marling & Lucas, 2009). Is it possible that language used by low-SES African-American parents in the study sounded harsh to the researchers but was in fact understood as child-affirming in the families that were observed? Might the idea of 'being nice' to children differ across cultures and languages?

5 In another critique of this research, Nation (n.d.) points out that low-SES parents are guarded in their speech when they are being observed, while the presence of researchers tends to have the opposite effect on high-SES parents. Given this reality, do you think we should dismiss the idea that low-SES children are less advantaged in terms of the quantity and quality of the language they hear at home? Why or why not?

Another factor that impacts children's vocabulary development is access to books and the literacy practices in the home; studies of both L1 and L2 vocabulary development confirm the importance of this factor. Uchikoshi (2006) investigated low-SES Spanish-speaking ELLs and found that the number of books in the home, whether in English or Spanish, was a good predictor of the children's English vocabulary knowledge. Uchikoshi (2014) also tested kindergarten-age ELLs on their ability to do things like identify the front of a book and point to print on the page, and found an association between the children's familiarity with books and their English vocabulary growth. Other studies of primary ELLs show that literacy-related activities, such as looking at books with children, reading books aloud, repeated readings, explaining words, telling stories, and helping with homework, have beneficial effects on L2 vocabulary development (Elley, 1989; Uchikoshi, 2014).

School Programs

Researchers have also investigated various kinds of school support programs for young learners of English and their impact on word learning. One widely implemented type of support in North America is pull-out ESL, which takes ELLs out of their English-medium mainstream classroom for part of the school day for special language instruction. Another alternative in the United States is Structured English Immersion (SEI), an intensive preparatory program which ELLs must complete before joining regular classes taught in English. A variety of bilingual education programs have also been widely implemented. Some are transitional, with the goal of preparing ELLs to join mainstream classrooms with English-only instruction. Others give both ELLs and L1 English speakers an opportunity to study school subjects in two languages over a longer time period.

Uchikoshi (2014) compared Spanish-speaking ELLs in early-exit transitional bilingual and mainstream classrooms over a three-year period. She found that learners in both programs made advances in their receptive knowledge of English vocabulary, but growth was more rapid in the bilingual program. However, learners in the bilingual programs were less proficient at the outset. For this reason, they had opportunities to meet and learn a greater number of high-frequency words that would typically occur repeatedly in the classroom language they were exposed to. This could explain why they learned more words over the three-year period than the more proficient learners. That is, the more proficient learners were less likely to have repeated encounters with the lower-frequency words that they still needed to learn. It is possible that this difference rather than the program type may explain the greater growth rate they experienced. The most striking difference between the groups was the steeper growth of L1 (Spanish) vocabulary knowledge in learners in the bilingual programs. Given the close connection between L1 and L2 vocabulary development (Cummins, 1979; Paradis, 2007), this bodes well for these learners' English vocabulary growth over time.

A large study of nearly 200 Spanish-speaking sixth graders enrolled in a variety of programs (including pull-out ESL, bilingual, and SEI) since kindergarten was specifically designed to investigate the effects of bilingual and English-only support (MacSwan, Thompson, Rolstad, McAlister, & Lobo, 2017). Not surprisingly, the researchers found that the learners' reading comprehension in English and knowledge of English vocabulary were important factors in their academic achievement in school subjects taught in English; this is an argument for any kind of support program that helps ELLs develop their knowledge of English. However, the most powerful predictor of academic performance in English proved to be learners' level of literacy in Spanish. Taken together, these findings constitute a strong argument for school programs designed to support young learners' knowledge of both first and second languages. As the researchers explain:

> Bilingual education contributes to children's success at school because it provides them with access to content-area knowledge so they can keep up academically during the time it takes them to learn English.
>
> (MacSwan et al., 2017, pp. 236–237)

Research also tells us that L1 literacy and the well-developed knowledge of L1 vocabulary that goes with it provide a rich resource for learning and remembering new L2 vocabulary.

The research on environmental factors discussed so far confirms commonsense intuitions: longer periods of exposure and advantaged family contexts are associated with greater L2 vocabulary growth for young ELLs. What may be more unexpected, however, are the indications that home speech input and literacy practices need not be in English to be effective in supporting English vocabulary development. We have also seen that rates of English vocabulary acquisition do not suffer when children study in bilingual programs, and that knowledge of the L1 supports academic achievement. All of this suggests that education policymakers and teachers do well to support primary ELLs' development in both L1 and L2.

Age and Cognition

Imagine that a five-year-old girl and her ten-year-old brother who both know no English arrive at school in an English-speaking country. Which one can we expect will learn L2 vocabulary more quickly? It is likely to be the big brother. Research shows that the age at which a learner first comes into contact with the L2 is important and that older primary learners tend to learn faster in school (Goldberg, Paradis, & Crago, 2008). We have seen that older learners are likely to have learned the vocabulary for many more concepts in their L1, creating a foundation for learning L2 vocabulary for concepts they already know. Older children are also more cognitively mature. That is, they are more able to do complex mental tasks like noticing a new word in spoken language and holding it in memory long enough to attend to clues about its meaning in the input (Nagy, 2005). Furthermore, older children are more metalinguistically aware. **Metalinguistic awareness** is the ability to reflect on language and manipulate it. For example, older children are more able to talk about words and define them or say what sounds are found in them (Lightbown & Spada, 2013). An important aspect of metalinguistic ability is **phonological awareness**; this involves understanding that spoken words are made up of sounds and syllables. If a child is asked to perform an operation such as removing the *b* at the beginning of *bring* and they can say that the resulting word is *ring*, this is an indicator of phonological awareness. L1 phonological awareness underlies L1 reading ability and often predicts L2 word reading skills. That is, a Spanish-speaking child with a high level of phonological awareness in Spanish is likely to be good at reading English words. This might be expected to apply to speakers of languages that use the Roman alphabet, but the connection has also been found in studies of speakers of languages such as Hebrew and Chinese that use non-Roman orthographies and are not typologically similar to English (Geva & Ramírez, 2015). Metalinguistic awareness also involves **morphological awareness**, the ability to see that words like *effortless* and *sunlight* are made up of two parts. We will look more closely at studies of morphological ability in the discussion of L1 influences below.

Older children are also likely to be faster L2 vocabulary learners because they have more L1 reading experience than younger children. With L1 reading experience come increases in the ability to use letter–sound correspondences to decode L1 words; there is evidence that L1 decoding ability is carried over into reading in the L2. For example, Durgunoğlu, Nagy, and Hancin-Bhatt (1993) showed that young Spanish-speaking learners of English who had strong L1 decoding skills were proficient at reading English words. Reading also brings more opportunities to learn new words by inferring their meanings. The increased knowledge of the world and expanded vocabulary size that come through L1 reading mean that the older learner has a larger set of semantic concepts available for linking to L2 word forms.

Researchers have also considered the role of factors related to differences in certain cognitive abilities. One mental capacity that is consistently associated with both L1 and L2 word learning ability is **phonological memory**. This mental attribute is measured using tasks that require the test taker to attend to and repeat non-words that are presented orally. For example, children might be assessed on their accuracy in repeating two-syllable non-words like *kabbit* and *megole*. The testing then moves on to ever more challenging three-, four-, and even five-syllable non-words like *consamponita* and *enpisonkerous* (examples from Farnia & Geva, 2011). This kind of memory ability is thought to be relevant to learning vocabulary because it means that a new word can be heard and held in memory, while learners are also using mental resources to attend to meaningful information in the context and forming hypotheses about its possible meaning. Farnia and Geva (2011) found that ELLs' phonological memory was positively associated with their receptive vocabulary development over the six years of primary school.

First Language

As discussed above, an important resource that children bring to the learning of English vocabulary is the experience of learning their L1. If the L1 has features in common with English, there are likely to be facilitating effects. We will explore this idea by looking at two very different languages—Spanish and Mandarin Chinese—and research that investigates the English vocabulary development of young L1 speakers of these languages. Activity 3.2 highlights one of the many differences between Spanish and Mandarin Chinese.

Activity 3.2

English has an abundance of **compound words** like *babysitter*, *newspaper*, and *heartfelt*. A compound is a combination of two or more words that function as a single unit of meaning. Sometimes, English compounds are hyphenated, as in the cases of *merry-go-round*, *ground-breaking*, and *five-year-old*. There are also open compounds in which the words appear separately; these can be considered collocations. Examples are *pencil sharpener*, *board game*, and *hamburger bun*. Recent additions to the vocabulary of English include many compounds pertaining to computer technology and social media. Examples are *screen saver*, *mousepad*, *text message*, *phone app*, and *Facebook*.

Compounding is an important word building process in Mandarin Chinese. Below are two sets of Mandarin Chinese compounds; note that each compound is made up of two characters.

高兴 – happy	注意 – note, pay attention
高档 – upscale	满意 – satisfied
高中 – high school	同意 – agree
高手 – master	意思 – meaning
高尚 – noble	愿意 – willing
高矮 – height	生意 – business, make a living

1 Identify the character that is shared among all the items in each set. You do not need to know Mandarin Chinese to do this.

2 Using the English definitions, try to guess the meaning of the shared character. (Answers appear at the end of the activity.)

3 Montreal English teacher Christine Que collected and analyzed a corpus of essays produced by Mandarin Chinese speakers in a university ESL course. She found they used more compounds in their writing than comparable L1 English university students and that some of their compounds were innovative and unconventional (Que & Horst, 2010). What do you think the writer's intention was in each of the following?

nutrition box   *rushing time*   *living pace*   *eater-lover*

housestyle food   *food habit*   *stress living*

4 Compounds are much less frequent in Spanish than in English, and this is reflected in learner productions. Try to guess the English compound that corresponds to each of the following phrases (from Hatch & Brown, 1995) produced by Spanish-speaking learners of English.

shoes for water ice

one man is for clean clothes

rooms for sleep

5 What are the implications of these cross-language differences for teaching English vocabulary?

6 Do you think primary school learners are aware of compounds in English? What might a learning activity focusing on English compounds for primary ESL learners look like?

Answers to questions 1 and 2:

In the first column, all the compounds contain 高 (gāo). This character can mean 'physically tall or high', but it is also used in a more abstract sense to refer to a higher level or status of someone/something. In the second column, all the compounds contain 意 (yì). This has many different meanings including 'idea', 'thought', 'wish', 'significance', and 'imply'. Its use in the sense of 'wish' or 'intent' seems most relevant to the compounds shown here.

(Wang, n.d.)

As Activity 3.2 illustrates, Mandarin Chinese and English both make use of compounding. However, while Mandarin Chinese uses a compound for a person who teaches (教员 = jiao yuan = teach person), English uses the derived forms *teacher* or *instructor*. That is, in English, nouns can be formed from the verbs *teach* and *instruct* by adding derivational suffixes like *-er* and *-or*. Derivation is an important process in English word formation as well as in Spanish. Thus, Spanish has the noun *instructor*, which is derived via suffixation from the root verb *instruir* (teach). Other derived forms in Spanish are *instrucción*, and *instruccional*, which correspond to English *instruction* and *instructional*. As in English, suffixes are used to convert a root form to different parts of speech. In Spanish, *-al* and *-oso* are adjective makers and *-ción* changes a verb into a noun. Derived forms are relatively scarce in Mandarin Chinese (Chen, Ramírez, Luo, Geva, & Ku, 2012).

These differences mean that young ELLs whose home language is Spanish have a great deal of exposure to derived words, while those who speak Chinese at home have relatively little. Conversely, Chinese learners of English have much more exposure to compounds than Spanish learners. How might home language experiences affect the ability of learners from these different backgrounds to deal with words in English such as *effortless* or *sunshine*? The question is worth asking because Spanish and Chinese are widely-spoken L1s in the ELL populations of the United States, Canada, and other English-speaking countries, and because of the implications for learning. Studies of young native speakers of English show that morphological awareness—the ability to break words into parts—is a key factor in vocabulary development and reading comprehension during the primary years (Lesaux & Kieffer, 2008).

Research confirms that Spanish-speaking primary school ELLs have an advantage over their Mandarin-Chinese-speaking classmates when it comes to learning derived words. That is, young Spanish speakers appear to be better at tasks like supplying the correct form of *magic* to complete 'The performer was a good _____'. There is also confirmation that Mandarin-Chinese-speaking primary ELLs have an advantage in learning compound words (Lam, Chen, Geva, Luo, & Li, 2012). But ELLs in both L1 groups appear to increase their awareness of both types of morphology during the primary years. As with L1 learners of English, developing morphological awareness matters because it gives the learner a useful strategy for guessing meanings. Derivational ability appears to be especially important (Ramírez et al., 2011). If the learner knows the root *effort* and other words ending with *-less*, and can break *effortless* into its parts, the learner can work out what it means. Morphological endings also assist learners in understanding sentences by providing clues to grammar. For example, knowing that *-ness* denotes a noun and *-ful* signifies an adjective can help readers interpret a sentence like 'There was more wickedness to come on that fateful day'.

Knowledge of Spanish also offers young ELLs the advantage of shared cognate vocabulary. For example, in the discussion above, we saw that both English and Spanish use the word *instructor* in the sense of *teacher* (Chen et al., 2012). In Chapter 1, we noted that English has borrowed many words from Latin and French; this means that speakers of French and other Latinate languages such as Spanish and Italian will recognize many English cognates. Spanish *instructor* and French *instructeur* are easy-to-see examples; other cognate connections such as English *screen* and French *écran* may not be so readily recognized; and as we will see, learners may need explicit guidance to help them identify these less transparent pairs. Indeed, in oral language, even exact cognates may not be recognized if their pronunciation differs substantially. For example, English *ocean* and French *océan* are essentially identical in their written form, but they would not necessarily be recognized in spoken language.

The availability of cognates offers a potentially powerful vocabulary advantage for Spanish-speaking learners of English. It is estimated that the two languages share over 10,000 cognates and that over a third of the English words in scientific texts are Spanish cognates (Chen et al., 2012). But learners need to be able to see these cross-language vocabulary connections in order for them to be useful. The question of **cognate awareness** in primary Spanish-speaking ELLs is the subject of several interesting studies. For example, Chen et al. (2012) explored morphological awareness in Chinese- and Spanish-speaking learners of English and also compared the cognate effect in these two populations. Chinese–English cognates are almost non-existent, so the cognate advantage was not available to the Chinese-speaking learners in the study. The researchers divided test words on the PPVT into Spanish–English cognates (for example, *gigantic* and *astronaut*) and non-cognates (for example, *climbing* and *digging*). The two L1 groups performed similarly on the non-cognate items, but the Spanish-speaking ELLs outperformed the Chinese speakers on the Spanish–English cognates. We can conclude, therefore, that the young Spanish speakers were able to exploit the cognate connection to build their knowledge of English vocabulary.

In a study that investigated fourth-, fifth-, and sixth-grade Spanish speakers, even the youngest learners proved to be able to find and circle Spanish–English cognates that occurred in English reading passages (Nagy, Garcia, Durgunoğlu, & Hancin-Bhatt, 1993). The learners who were better at identifying the cognates scored higher on a measure of comprehension of the passages. This link to reading comprehension is important, as it shows that successful cognate identification can be deployed in real language use. However, the research also showed that the learners seriously under-identified the cognates; they circled less than half. The researchers concluded that ability to recognize cognates can be substantially enhanced by awareness-raising instruction.

White and Horst (2012) investigated the use of a set of five activities designed to raise cognate awareness with French-speaking learners of English (aged 9 to 10 years) over a period of ten weeks. The learners were asked to look for possible cognate words in reading passages, and they worked on generating 'rules' for less easy-to-recognize French–English cognate patterns (for example, in *strange/étrange, stomach/estomac,* and *spirit/esprit,* the pattern is: English *s* = French *e* or *é*). Learners in comparable classes worked with the same reading activities, but the vocabulary focus was on antonyms and no connections to French were made. The researchers found that students in the groups that received the cognate awareness activities had substantially higher levels of cognate awareness than the students who participated in the antonym activities—as indicated by answers to questions that probed cognate awareness such as the following: 'If you know the word *pile* in French, does it help you to understand the word *pile* in English?' Classroom Snapshot 3.1 is an excerpt of an interview with one of the teachers who participated in the research (Horst, White, & Bell, 2010).

Classroom Snapshot 3.1

Faye is a teacher of fourth- and fifth-grade French-speaking learners of English in Montreal. She implemented experimental activities designed to raise learners' awareness of French–English cognates (available on the ALERT website; see Appendix). One of the activities involved identifying cognates in a simple passage about the Norman Conquest of Britain, an event that brought many French loanwords into English. Another focused on a pattern of cognate resemblance that may not be easy to recognize (*étudiant/student, écran/screen, ésprit/spirit*). The children also wrote reflective journals about the cognate activities. Faye responded to the experience in an interview.

Interviewer: What about the cognates?
Faye: I really enjoyed this because even though we often make reference to words that are very similar in French and English, I don't have any activities prepared so what I really enjoyed was the story of William of Normandy … Now this I loved, also for the cultural and historical aspect of it and it was just really interesting.
Interviewer: Did the students love it as well?
Faye: I think they did. Personally, I was amazed when I first did the highlighting of all the words in the text. I couldn't believe how many were so similar, and after we did these activities it came up often in class—well, what's this word in English? Well, it's the same word, it's a cognate, remember? So it gave us an occasion to refer back to these activities.

Interviewer:	Do you think teachers are often kind of negative when they talk about cognates? When a child makes a mistake, say, because they use the word *sensible* to mean *sensitive* (= French *sensible*), the teacher might say, well, not all words are the same?
Faye:	Of course, when they say *library* and they mean *bookstore* (= French *librairie*), that jumps out at you. I think it's a realization that there are so many words that <u>can</u> help them. And we teach strategies like 'guess intelligently', 'guess meaning from context.' So 'Does the word look like a French word?' definitely fits into strategy training.
Interviewer:	Do you think they understand more difficult cognates, for example *school* (= French *école*)?
Faye:	They got that!
Interviewer:	In their journals, a couple of your kids actually said things along the lines of 'school = école' … Once they saw the pattern—words like *scarlet* (= French *écarlate*)—do you think that helped the kids?
Faye:	I really do. I really like cognates. For me, it was an eye-opener and for them, I think there were little light bulbs going off, they were like 'Oh, that's kind of cool' …
Interviewer:	Possibly some of them saw it as a kind of puzzle; they could decode it.
Faye:	Exactly.

In this interview, we see that both the teacher and the students were surprised to discover how many helpful cognates were available. Research shows that this valuable resource is often underused (Lightbown & Libben, 1984; Otwinowska, 2016). The problem of 'false friends' was also noted in the interview. French-speaking learners of English may say *library* when they mean *bookstore* because the cognate connection is misleading: French *librairie* means bookstore. A famous example of a Spanish–English false cognate pair is Spanish *embarazado*, which looks and sounds like English *embarrassed* but actually means *pregnant*. The problem of false cognates is real but should not be overestimated. Making cognate connections may lead to occasional errors, but it remains an effective strategy because in the large majority of cases, cognates are true friends (Chen et al., 2012). Arguably, French–English *library/librairie* is a case of near friends rather than false friends, as both refer to places where books are found.

In this section, we examined factors that have an influence on L2 vocabulary acquisition. Some of these can be seen as accidents of birth and circumstance. Thus, a very fortunate child may have the gifts of a strong mind, a comfortable economic situation, rich opportunities to develop L1 vocabulary, a large amount of exposure to the new language at school, and a home language that has many features in common with English, while another child might not be advantaged in the same ways. There may be little scope for instruction to impact these 'given' characteristics. But there is a great deal that educators can do in the areas related to cognition and language awareness. Teachers can work to develop learners' metalinguistic awareness by highlighting words and talking about them (for example, see Classroom Snapshot 2.2 on page 65). They can promote morphological awareness by helping learners dissect compound and derived words into their constituent parts. And they can raise awareness of cognate connections between words in English and the language the learners already know. First languages like Spanish and French may lend themselves to this more than Chinese and Korean, but most of the world's languages share some words with English. English words related to sports and technology, for example, have been borrowed into many other languages. Bilingual teachers who know the learners' L1 have an advantage when it comes to identifying cognates or borrowed words, but any teacher can ask, 'Does this sound like a word in your language?'

L2 Word Knowledge in Development

Many of the studies we have examined so far assessed primary school learners' vocabulary size in terms of their ability to point to pictures in response to spoken words or to name pictures. Studies using tests with picture tasks such as the PPVT have resulted in important findings. They have shown that ELLs' vocabulary continues to grow over the primary years, and that there is a strong and consistent connection between L2 vocabulary size and L2 reading comprehension. Researchers have tested both accuracy and speed of performance on picture tasks and shown that accuracy continues to increase and response times decrease as ELLs move into the high school years (Goldberg, Paradis, & Crago, 2008). But as we saw in Chapter 1, there are other kinds of word knowledge; the ability to link a word form to an object or concept is just one aspect of what it means to know the word. In this section, we explore other aspects of ELLs' developing knowledge, beginning with a look at their use of English vocabulary in speaking and writing.

Productive Vocabulary in Use

In 1992, Harley observed that L2 learners' initial use of vocabulary tends to be imprecise. She found that English-speaking students of various ages (Grades 1, 4, and 10) learning French in immersion classes used overly general words in their speech in comparison to L1 French-speaking peers of the same age. For example, the L2 learners produced phrases like the French equivalent of 'he *goes* into the water', instead of the more precise *plonger* (dive). They appear to be stretching limited lexical resources by using the general all-purpose (or GAP) word *go* to stand in for a word they do not know. In studies of adult L2 writing, this use of familiar all-purpose words, where more specific terms would be more native-like, has been referred to as reliance on 'lexical teddy bears' (Hasselgren, 1994). Goldberg, Paradis, and Crago (2008) investigated the GAP-word phenomenon with early primary ELLs in Edmonton, Canada. Over a two-year period, they interviewed the young immigrant learners five times and noted their use of the verb *do*. The initial interviews featured uses like 'He do ribbit, ribbit', and 'He do a baseball'. Much as Harley (1992) found, these learners of English relied on *do* to compensate for their lack of knowledge of the more specific verbs *say* and *throw*. By the final interview, the over-extensions of *do* had decreased significantly. This is likely due to the learners' increased productive vocabulary size as they learned the more specific verbs they needed to express their ideas.

Young learners' productive vocabulary development was explored in a **lexical richness** study, described in Spotlight Study 3.2. Horst and Collins (2006) predicted that the learners' writing would become ever more lexically rich over time. That is, they expected that as learners acquired knowledge of more specific words, the proportion of high-frequency words like *do*, *make*, and *have* in their written productions would decrease and proportions of less-frequent words would increase. However, the study delivered some unexpected results.

Spotlight Study 3.2

Horst and Collins (2006) investigated French-speaking learners of English in their sixth year of schooling (11–12 year-olds) in Quebec. Although English is the majority language in the rest of Canada, French is the main language of Quebec. Like most children in the province, the learners in this study attended French-medium schools and had little exposure to English outside of English class. All were taking part in special intensive ESL programs in which they devoted approximately 400 hours in their Grade 6 year to the learning of English. The regular Grade 6 curriculum (science, mathematics, French language arts, etc.) was completed in French in a condensed format to free up time for the intensive English program.

The young learners were asked to write narrative texts in response to picture prompts after each of the four 100-hour intervals of intensive English language instruction. They were encouraged to supply a French word if an English word they needed was not known. Over the course of the study, students made considerable progress in listening and speaking. However, when the writing was analyzed using lexical frequency profiling software on the Lextutor website (see Appendix), the expected increase in use of less frequent English word families was not found. Instead, the learners were using ever larger proportions of words from the list of the 1,000 most frequent word families.

What was the explanation for this unexpected result? The writing samples were clearly improving over time. For example, one learner produced the following at the beginning of the study (English translations of French words have been added):

> My grandmother is sick. Why? I don't no. She have begin to sick the night of November 13. We haven't *assez* [= enough] of dollars to help my grandmother. I'm very sad. It's not just for she and for me! I thing *que* [= that] for my cat: Lady, is sick. It not eat and is *faible* [= weak] …

By the end of the study, she was able to produce these relatively fluent lines:

> My story is in a school yard. Yannick and his friends play soccer on the grass. The have fun. Laura is there too but she can't play soccer because the boys don't want a girl in their team. Laura is angry because she know that the boys lets play Yannick: You and your friends are just macho! …

A close re-examination of the writing revealed signs of lexical progress not captured in the initial analysis. First, as the sample above illustrates, there was heavy reliance on French in the earlier writing, but instances of using French words to fill lexical gaps decreased over the four measurement intervals. Second, cognate analysis revealed that the students' writing featured fewer overly formal words borrowed from their mother tongue. For instance, in an early story, one learner had written: 'He is thinking about the *sensation* that the boy can have in his heart the next day.' Later productions tended to use fewer French–English cognates like *sensation* and more basic English words like *feelings*. This greater use of simpler, more age-appropriate vocabulary appears to account for the increase in proportions of 1,000-level words. Third, although the learners continued to use high-frequency words, there was greater variety; word family counts showed that numbers of different 1,000-level families used in the stories increased. Finally, there was an increase in morphological complexity. Types-per-family analysis showed that learners were more able to use inflected and derived forms of a word like *believe* (for example, *belief, believes, believing, believer*).

Like studies using picture-naming tasks, this study shows that learners' productive vocabulary size increases over time. In this case, the learners were increasingly able to write English words that corresponded to the concepts they wished to express. The study provides evidence of development in two additional aspects of vocabulary knowledge: register and word parts. That is, the students were more able to use words at the appropriate level of formality and they used more inflected and derived forms.

The corpus methodology of this study involved using computer tools to identify overall patterns of vocabulary development that would probably be difficult for human evaluators to detect (see Chapter 1 for other examples of corpus-informed vocabulary research). Each of the 210 participants wrote four narratives; these were taken together to form a learner corpus of over 80,000 words that could then be analyzed using lexical frequency profiling software and other tools, such as a cognate indexer. Another strength of the study is its longitudinal design; this made it possible to investigate patterns of development over time. However, the profiling tools used in this study assessed the learners' writing in terms of words found on frequency lists that are based on large corpora of adult language. Arguably, an analysis based on word frequencies in the classroom input the learners were exposed to (teachers' language, pedagogical materials, their classmates' language) might be a more suitable measure of the students' success in learning the words that were available to learn.

Vocabulary Depth

In contrast to vocabulary size studies that investigate how many words ELLs know, studies of vocabulary depth focus on how well words are known. The relationship between deep knowledge of English vocabulary and performance on measures of reading comprehension is well established. One way of assessing depth involves exploring the extent to which learners know the various senses of polysemous words. In one study, August et al. (2005) asked fourth-grade ELLs and native English-speakers to judge whether the following sentences featuring different meanings of *grow* made sense:

We were growing sheep last year.

Their love for each other grew.

The boy grew two inches.

My teacher wants the homework to grow.

The learners were also given a production task in which they were asked to write as many meanings as they could think of for the words *bug, ring, light,* and *hand*. Higher scores were given to responses that were more distant from the core meaning. For instance, in defining *bug*, the response 'a bug in a computer program' was given a higher score than 'insect', which is the core meaning. Comparisons to English-speaking learners of the same age showed that performance on both measures was lower in the ELL group.

A similar finding is reported in a study of young Turkish-speaking immigrant learners of Dutch in primary schools in the Netherlands. Verhallen and Schoonen (1993) asked the children to talk about the Dutch equivalents of words like *nose, alarm clock,* and *secret.* The extensive oral interviews probed their ability to provide definitions and also asked them to describe the appearance of the object, the things one can do with it, and the various kinds that exist. The researchers observed that category language was often missing in the L2 learner definitions; that is, the L1 Dutch speakers were more likely to say that a nose is a body part.

Overall, performance of the young Turkish speakers lagged considerably behind that of Dutch-speaking children of the same age. But when older Turkish-speaking children whose Dutch vocabulary size matched that of the young Dutch-speaking children were investigated, the differences disappeared. This finding is consistent with other research indicating that vocabulary depth and vocabulary size go hand in hand (Goldberg, Paradis, & Crago, 2008). Some researchers (Vermeer, 2001) have questioned whether they should be considered separate entities. Certainly, it is reasonable to expect that the ability to explain meanings in depth and make connections to other L2 words relies on being able to draw on a large store of known L2 vocabulary; we will return to this point in Chapter 4.

Teaching the Vocabulary of School

Researchers and educators have created teaching approaches designed to address the vocabulary shortfall so many studies of ELLs have detailed. The focus is on the academic vocabulary needed for reading and learning subject matter at school. As we will see, these instructional approaches follow a multifaceted approach based on research discussed earlier in this chapter.

The designers of research-informed instruction agree that vocabulary teaching is at its most effective when teachers exploit classroom reading materials to teach new words in context. Published storybooks are a good source of new vocabulary for learners in the early grades because they are usually richer in vocabulary than the materials designed to teach learners how to read. While stories are appealing to learners, they tend to contain fewer of the academic words older primary school learners need to know.

This is an argument for selecting informational texts for in-depth vocabulary work with middle- and upper-primary learners. Beck, McKeown, and Kucan (2005) suggest that teachers first read the text aloud and explain any difficult words briefly along the way. Then, after the children are familiar with the content, teachers can attend to selected vocabulary in greater depth, drawing on the content to enrich learners' understanding of the words.

Selecting Words

In this section, we consider two principled ways of selecting words to teach. The first relies on teacher judgments while the second makes use of Greene and Coxhead's (2015) MSVL.

Informed Judgment

A well-known way of selecting the most useful words to teach in a story or textbook is the three-tier system proposed by Beck et al. (2005). Their focus is on at-risk learners—both L1 English speakers and ELLs—and they prioritize academic vocabulary that supports the study of school subjects. Applying the scheme involves assigning the words of a text to one of three 'tiers'; judgments are based on the teacher's intuitions about students' needs and abilities. The Tier 1 category is made up of words that do not need to be taught because they are likely to be well known to children whose first language is English through conversational interactions in the home and at play. Examples are *clock*, *baby*, and *happy*. Knowledge of such words is consistent with Cummins' (2008) notion of basic interpersonal communicative skills (BICS). But it cannot be assumed that young learners of English will know all of the Tier 1 words in a text, so some words from this category may be good candidates for teaching in classes with ELLs (Calderón et al., 2005).

Tier 3 words are at the other end of the usefulness spectrum in the scheme. They are low-frequency words such as *isotope*, *lathe*, and *peninsula* that typically occur in a specialist domain and are unlikely to be met often outside of that domain. *Isotope*, for example, may be encountered in materials for older learners studying chemistry, but it is highly unlikely to occur frequently in reading across the primary school curriculum. Because of the limited usefulness of Tier 3 words, primary teachers need not devote valuable classroom time to teaching them. A short explanation will suffice if a Tier 3 word stands in the way of comprehending the content of a text.

According to Beck et al. (2005), Tier 2 words are the ideal targets for instruction; these are words judged to fall between the two extremes. They give *coincidence*, *absurd*, and *industrious* as examples of Tier 2 words suitable for teaching to fourth graders. Tier 2 words should be frequent words that are likely to be met across a variety of school subjects; that is, learners will be able to use them in situations beyond the context in which they are first encountered. Tier 2 vocabulary is consistent with Cummins' (2008) idea of cognitive academic language proficiency (CALP).

Researchers who have focused more specifically on the needs of ELLs give additional selection guidelines: words chosen for in-depth instruction should be central to understanding the text. Ideally, they are also used repeatedly, as this gives students multiple opportunities to see the word in use. In the discussion of incidental vocabulary learning in Chapter 2, we saw that learners may need to meet a new word eight or more times in their reading in order for it to be remembered. Words with multiple meanings are good candidates because they help learners see how words function in different subject domains. For example, as we observed in Chapter 1, *volume* has different meanings in mathematics, science, and language arts classes. The researchers also recommend choosing words with affixes; these can be exploited for raising awareness of morphology. Where possible, it is suggested that teachers choose words that have cognate relationships across languages spoken by the learners so that they can gain experience in recognizing cognates (Carlo et al., 2004).

Corpus-Informed Selection

An alternative to making careful human judgments is to let technology do the job. Greene and Coxhead (2015) created the Middle School Vocabulary Lists (MSVL) precisely for the purpose of identifying the frequently used academic words that are important for young learners to know in the later years of their primary schooling. The lists are based on the analysis of over a hundred sixth-, seventh-, and eighth-grade textbooks used in public schools in the United States. As detailed in Chapter 1, there are lists of words for each of five subject areas: 1) English grammar and writing, 2) health, 3) mathematics, 4) science, and 5) social studies and history. The five lists do not include words on the lists of the 2,000 most frequent English families, as these can be considered Tier 1 words that are likely to be familiar. To locate the MSVL words in a school text, a teacher can enter the passage into the profiling software available on the Lextutor website and the MSVL words in the text will be highlighted automatically (see Activity 1.3 on page 22 for detailed instructions). The output will also show which MSVL words are repeated in the text and the morphological variants that are used.

A strong argument for focusing in-depth teaching on MSVL vocabulary is its coverage power (see Chapter 1 for more on coverage). On average, 1 in 13 words found in middle school textbooks is an MSVL word. Clearly, this is vocabulary that learners will meet again at school. A large proportion of MSVL words are also found on the Academic Word List (AWL), a list of words that occur frequently in university textbooks. Selecting words to teach using the MSVL has the advantage of removing the guesswork from a decision-making process that may be challenging and time consuming. Teachers in a study of in-depth vocabulary instruction reported being pleased to have the 'insurmountable task' of word selection and activity design done for them by the researchers (Calderón et al., 2005, p. 130).

Selection that draws on the strengths of both methods is probably the best solution. Automated selection can be used to identify MSVL words in a text, but teacher judgments are needed to determine which of these may already be known by a particular group of learners and which are most useful to the topic or task at hand. Teacher input is also needed to select words that lend themselves to raising learners' awareness of morphology and cognate connections. Activity 3.3 provides an opportunity to explore both methods of selection.

Activity 3.3

Read the sample science text below. It is considered suitable for third graders (Baker et al., 2014, p. 35).

1 As you read, circle words that you judge to be academic vocabulary suited to in-depth instruction. Use criteria discussed in the previous section on 'Informed Judgment'. Try to identify about ten words, as researchers agree that more than ten is too many for in-depth treatment of the words in lessons for primary learners (Baker et al., 2014).

2 If possible, compare your choices to those of your colleagues and discuss your decisions. Narrow your choices to about six words.

3 Compare your selection to that of a third-grade teacher, which appears after the text below. Do you agree with her choices? How reliable is this selection process in your view? Does it matter if there is disagreement?

4 The text was analyzed using the VocabProfile MSVL tool available on the Lextutor website (see Appendix). Words found on the MSVL science list appear below. How effective is the tool for identifying suitable academic words in your view? Are there any words that you did not identify? Among the MSVL words, are there any words you would not include on your list of teaching targets? Why?

Sample science text
When you walk into a zoo today, the exhibits look different than they used to look years ago. Before the 1960s, zoos had cages with tile walls and floors. Now, animals in zoos live in more natural environments. For example, instead of enormous gorillas pacing back and forth in cramped cement areas, they play on soft grass and nap in trees. Before, large birds lived in small cages. Now, zoos have large exhibits where birds can stretch their wings and soar from tree to tree. According to zoo design expert Jon C. Coe, these changes often have a positive impact on animals' health and happiness.

Still, creating better living spaces is just one step toward improving the lives of animals that live in zoos. Even in exhibits that look like their natural environments, animals can become bored. According to Coe, boredom can have harmful effects.

'An exhibit may look great, but it isn't doing much for the animal unless it also involves a choice of things to do all day,' said Coe. Animals need to be challenged with activities such as looking for food and exploring their surroundings. In fact, some research has shown that giving zoo animals more options and activities promotes good health and lowers the incidence of violent behavior. Today, several zoos have created living environments for their animals that involve the kinds of pursuits that Coe described. For instance, the orangutans at the National Zoo in Washington, DC, can travel across the zoo on overhead ropes to visit friends.

Coe recommends more investigation into these types of zoo exhibits and their impact on animal health. With this new pursuit of creating more natural environments in zoo exhibits, he sees a happier and healthier future for many zoo animals.

Teacher-selected words:

environment, exhibit, investigation, impact, pursuit, options

The teacher considered *natural* and *design* but decided that the students were familiar with these. *Environment* and *investigation* were chosen because of their usefulness across subject areas. *Exhibit* and *pursuit* are repeated and are important for comprehending the text. She selected *exhibit* and *option* because of their morphological variants. *Impact, investigation,* and *option* are Spanish–English cognates.

MSVL-Science headwords:

area, challenge, create, design, enormous, environment, exhibit, impact, incidence, instance, investigation, involve, option, positive, research

Teaching Academic Vocabulary

Studies of large-scale programs of in-depth vocabulary instruction for primary ELLs in the United States have converged on a set of specific teaching practices that are associated with substantial word learning outcomes and gains in reading comprehension (Baker et al., 2014). The researchers recommend a text-based approach that focuses on five to eight words over the course of several days.

The first step is to read the passage with the students and explain the target vocabulary by providing student-friendly definitions that include examples and non-examples, and, if possible, concrete representations such as pictures and diagrams. It is important to link words back to the original reading passage. If the target word is *exhibit* and the class is working with the zoo passage in Activity 3.3, the teacher can refer to the new and old kinds of zoo exhibits discussed in the reading. The researchers recommend activities that promote elaborative processing such as making word maps. The word map shown in Figure 3.1 is an example developed in a first-grade class for the word *enormous*. The inclusion of examples, synonyms, antonyms, and non-examples consolidates definitional knowledge and helps build the multiple associations that contribute to vocabulary depth.

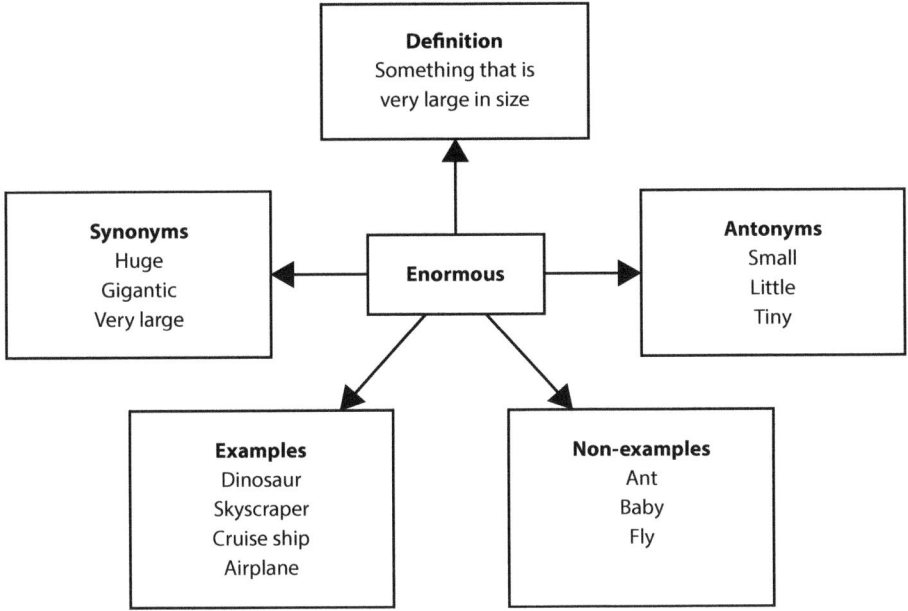

Figure 3.1 Word map for *enormous* (from Baker et al., 2014, p. 19)

A second activity type involves asking students questions that require them to show a more nuanced understanding of the meanings of words and their use in sentences. For example, students can be asked to examine the use of *exhibit* in contexts such as the following and identify the noun and verb uses.

We're going to see a special robotics <u>exhibit</u> at the Museum of Technology.
The bees <u>exhibited</u> signs of weakness and exhaustion.

They can also be asked to respond to questions such as 'If you saw an *exhibit*, would you have been at a museum or at the movies?' (Baker et al., 2014, p. 20). These recognition activities implement the principle of elaboration discussed in Chapter 2. That is, the students are engaged with the word in ways that go beyond its use in the original passage. The next step is to move learners in the direction of producing their own novel uses of the word. This can happen in a discussion of arguments for and against zoo exhibits of caged animals and in activities that encourage them to express opinions and share personal experiences related to the target word—orally and in writing. The researchers also emphasize retrieval activities that increase learners' exposure to the target words. This can take the form of games, puzzles, drawing activities, and review of previously taught words.

The final recommendation is to promote learners' ability to work out the meanings of unknown words independently through the teaching of three word learning strategies. One recommended strategy that we have examined closely in this chapter is the use of cognate clues. Many cognate resemblances may be easy to recognize; it is useful to show learners how to look for the less apparent cross-linguistic resemblances and encourage them to be confident in their guesses. Research also supports a second strategy discussed in this chapter: building learners' morphological awareness. Classroom Snapshot 3.2 shows how a primary teacher trains learners to use word part strategies to determine the meanings of new words.

Classroom Snapshot 3.2

Ms Ambrosi writes the word *unreachable* on the board. She tells students that the first thing she is going to do is to see whether she can find a root word. She breaks the word into three parts by drawing lines: *un|reach|able*. She illustrates that, after removing the affixes, they are left with the root word *reach*. She defines *reach*. She then calls on students to explain the meaning of the prefix *un-* (not) and the suffix *-able* (being capable of doing something) that they have already learned. Finally, she integrates the meaning of the root word and the affixes. She tells her students: '*Reach* means moving your hand or arm to try to touch or grab something. *Able* means you can do something. Then, the meaning of *reachable* is that you can touch or grab something. When we add the prefix *un-*, which means *not*, it changes the meaning of the word to *not being able to touch or grab something*. So, if I were trying to change a light bulb on the ceiling without a ladder, it would be *unreachable*.'

Ms Ambrosi continues by applying the procedure to other meanings of *reach* (for example, reaching a destination, reaching someone, reaching an agreement). In addition to teaching the meaning of the academic word *unreachable* using the word parts, Ms Ambrosi also discusses the word's morphological forms (i.e. *reach, reachable, unreachable*) in terms of their syntactical structure (i.e. verb, noun, adjective, adverb). The students then record the morphological forms according to their part of speech and function in sentences in their graphic organizer (see Table 3.1).

(Baker et al., 2014, p. 23)

VERBS (Action)	NOUNS (Person, place, thing, or idea)	ADJECTIVES (Words to describe nouns)	ADVERBS (Words to describe actions)
Investigate	Investigation Investigator	Investigative	
Exhibit	Exhibit Exhibition		
	Environment	Environmental	Environmentally
Pursue	Pursuit	Pursuant	
Opt	Option	Optional	Optionally
Reach	Reach	Unreachable Reachable	

Table 3.1 Graphic organizer (from Baker et al., 2014, p. 23)

The third recommended strategy for dealing with unfamiliar words is the use of contextual clues in the surrounding text to arrive at meanings. It is important to model this strategy with primary school learners by thinking aloud (Baker et al., 2014; Baumann, Font, Edwards, & Boland, 2005). To illustrate, we will consider the word *environment* and its use in the sample science text in Activity 3.3. Because *environment* occurs four times, we can expect to find useful clues to meaning. The first use in the text is as follows:

> Now, animals in zoos live in more natural *environments*. For example, instead of enormous gorillas pacing back and forth in cramped cement areas, they play on soft grass and nap in trees. Before, large birds lived in small cages.
>
> (Baker et al., 2014, p. 35)

The teacher can read out these sentences, ask the students to think about what *environment* means, and then model the guessing process as follows:

> I see some examples that can help me understand *environment*. A cement area is an environment and soft grass and trees are environments, too. A cage can be an environment for a bird. I think *environment* means 'place where an animal lives' or 'surroundings'. Let's read the sentences again and put *surroundings* in the place of *environment*. Do you think it fits?

Guidelines for contextual guessing with primary school learners need not be complicated: students can simply be directed to read around an unfamiliar word and look for clues. As the students become more familiar with the process, they can think aloud together in class, but they need guided practice before they will be able to implement the strategy independently (Baker et al., 2014; Baumann et al., 2005). Because naturally occurring contexts are not always as helpful as in the example of *environment* above (Beck, McKeown, & McCaslin, 1983), teachers should select the words and contexts used in practice activities judiciously (and warn students that the strategy might not always work). In order for ELLs to benefit from the strategy practice, they will first need to be able to easily understand the words in the sentence contexts and explanations. The 'think-aloud' above would have little to offer ELLs who did not understand the meanings of *cement*, *grass*, *cage*, and *surroundings*. Research discussed in Chapter 2 shows that for L2 learners to be able to comprehend texts and guess new word meanings on their own, the reading materials should contain no more than 1 new word in 50.

Summary

In this chapter, we saw that primary ELLs can make impressive gains in their knowledge of English words. Factors that support L2 word learning include socioeconomically advantaged family situations, ample amounts of exposure to the new language, increases in cognitive ability that come with maturation, and knowledge of a first language that has many features in common with English. An important and perhaps unexpected finding is the role of well-developed L1 knowledge; research shows that it is a strong predictor of vocabulary growth in English. We also saw that word learning means more than making increasing numbers of correct word-to-picture matches on the PPVT; primary ELLs are able to use new words productively in ways that demonstrate increasing depth of knowledge. But even though they may make large, rapid gains, ELLs' word knowledge usually lags behind that of their L1 English classmates. Teaching that targets the academic vocabulary of school is important in addressing this shortfall. This chapter outlined ways of selecting academic words; it also described effective research-informed instruction that promotes elaborative learning and focuses on both words and strategies for understanding and learning new words. We will return to these themes in the discussion of middle school and secondary school learners in Chapter 4.

4

Vocabulary Acquisition in Adolescent Learners of English

Preview

In this chapter, we begin with a look at who adolescent learners are and how they differ from younger learners in terms of the vocabulary growth they achieve at school. We will also examine the cognitive characteristics of adolescent learners and the new kinds of knowledge and abilities their more fully developed cognition supports. One of the challenges that many adolescent learners of English around the world face is low levels of vocabulary knowledge. Fortunately, ambitious programs of instruction have been designed to tackle these deficits. As we will see, some of the work falls to teachers, but strategies that empower learners to grow their vocabulary knowledge on their own are also part of the solution.

Adolescent Learners of English

In this book, adolescent learners are defined as students who are approximately 12 to 18 years old. In the United States, students in this age group attend middle and high school. Middle school students are typically in their 6th to 8th years of schooling. Many adolescents study English in schools around the world. In the 26 non-English speaking countries of the European Union, over 95% of secondary students studied English as a compulsory subject at school in 2015 (Eurostat, 2017). In 2010, the number of learners of English in China was estimated at an astounding 400 million; certainly many of these learners are secondary school students (Bolton & Graddol, 2012).

Adolescent ELLs also represent a substantial population in American public schools. Over a third of the 4.6 million ELLs in the school year 2014–15 were adolescents; this amounts to over 1.5 million students. The overwhelming majority of adolescent ELLs in the United States are Spanish speakers (NCES, 2018). There is a large adolescent learner population in Britain as well; in England, one in eight secondary students in publicly funded schools in 2013 did not have English as a first language. The most widely spoken first languages were Punjabi, Urdu, and Bengali (NALDIC, n.d.).

In United States schools, reported counts probably underestimate the true situation because students identified as ELLs when they entered primary school have often made considerable progress in spoken English by the time they reach middle or high school. They may have been able to perform well on tests of English, leading to their being classified as 'proficient' and no longer in need of ESL instruction. In addition, teachers and school administrators may assume that students who have good oral skills need no further language support to succeed academically, and the students themselves may no longer wish to be identified as ESL learners (NCES, 2018).

In a wide-ranging report on the academic literacy of adolescent ELLs in the United States, Short and Fitzsimmons (2007) outline the characteristics of this diverse group. Adolescent ELLs vary greatly in terms of levels of proficiency in English and their first languages. Many have low levels of L1 literacy, but this is not always the case. At the time of Short and Fitzsimmons' study, over half of the adolescent ELLs in American schools were reported to have been born in the United States, but many were found not to be proficient in English even after many years of schooling. The researchers also highlight the double learning challenge that newly arrived immigrant ELLs face: they must learn the English language and master academic content in English. They are expected to do both more quickly than their younger peers—often with less school support for their language learning than is available to primary school learners.

Indeed, the overall picture Short and Fitzsimmons (2007) paint is discouraging. Poverty is widespread in this population; United States census data for 2000 showed that over half of adolescent ELLs lived in families with incomes below the poverty line. In an investigation of reading skills in English, only a quarter of eighth-grade ELLs were found to perform at the level of proficient or above on a standard school measure. In other words, three quarters of the students performed at the most basic level. About two thirds of the ELLs who started high school in the ninth grade graduated four years later according to data for United States public schools in 2013–14 (NCES, 2015). This is well under the 82% graduation rate in the general population. Clearly, many adolescent ELLs in American schools are in crisis.

There is consensus that a strong and constantly growing knowledge of English vocabulary is key to developing the academic literacy that is crucial to learners' school success. In this chapter, we will examine factors that contribute to adolescents' L2 English vocabulary development and explore studies of effective instructional practices.

English Vocabulary Growth in Adolescents

This section begins with a look at vocabulary development in middle and secondary school, beginning with investigations of receptive vocabulary size. As discussed in Chapter 1, vocabulary size is defined as the number of word families that learners can recognize and associate with a simple definition. Size information is useful in determining long-term goals and delineating learners' development over time. Measures of vocabulary size can also be used diagnostically to help teachers identify the vocabulary their students most need to learn.

How Much? How Fast?

In Chapter 3, we saw that children's knowledge of English vocabulary is often assessed using the Peabody Picture Vocabulary Test (PPVT), a measure that asks learners to match spoken words to pictures. A young learner's performance on the PPVT is reported relative to age or grade norms; in other words, the test is not designed to estimate how many English word families the child actually knows. However, Biemiller and Slonim (2001) were able to investigate the vocabulary sizes of hundreds of primary school learners using interviews in which the children were asked to explain words of various levels of difficulty; older primary learners wrote explanatory sentences. Using this laborious methodology, Biemiller (2005) determined that by the end of sixth grade, the average vocabulary size of L1 English-speaking children in American schools amounts to 10,000 English word families.

An efficient alternative to this measurement process is the use of tests that rely on the corpus-informed lists of frequent English words that were discussed in Chapter 1. These innovative and powerful instruments have been used in many investigations of adolescent and adult learners of English. Until recently, corpus-informed size tests were not suited for use with very young learners because they required reading. The Picture Vocabulary Size Test (PVST), a recently developed picture test suitable for use with children and preliterate learners of English, was discussed in Chapter 3.

Frequency-based vocabulary size tests require test takers to indicate their knowledge of a tested word by matching it to a simple definition. Or, in the case of checklist tests such as *V_YesNo* (Meara & Miralpeix, 2016; see Appendix), the test taker simply indicates whether a tested word is known. The key feature of all frequency-based size testing is the sampling of words from frequency bands, which allows for extrapolations to all of the words in the band. For example, a learner who supplies correct answers to 70% of test items taken from the list of the 1,000 most frequent English word families is assumed to know 700 of these families. Performance on words in subsequent frequency bands—2,000, 3,000, 4,000, and so on—can be used to arrive at an estimate of the learner's overall vocabulary size.

Frequency-based size testing is an important innovation because learners' scores can be directly linked to known vocabulary goals such as the 5,000 families needed for comprehension of speech on an academic topic (van Zeeland, 2014) or the 8,000 needed for reading newspapers (Nation, 2006). Test outcomes provide concrete information about the words learners have mastered and the vocabulary they most need to study and learn. Vocabulary size instruments are regularly re-examined and improved. A recent measure that is principled in its design and easy to use is the updated edition of the Vocabulary Levels Test (VLT) by Webb, Sasao, and Ballance (2017; available on the Western University website, see Appendix).

Activity 4.1 features five questions from the Vocabulary Size Test (VST) by Nation and Beglar (2007). The questions sample families from the 20,000 frequency level, which is the most advanced level assessed by this version of the VST (monolingual, 20,000, Version A).

Activity 4.1

Test your knowledge! Answers appear at the end of the activity.

1 **sagacious:** She had many ideas that were **sagacious**.
   a instinctively clever
   b ridiculous and wild
   c about abusing people and being abused
   d rebellious and dividing

2 **spatiotemporal:** My theory is **spatiotemporal**.
   a focused on small details
   b annoying to people
   c objectionably modern
   d oriented to time and space

3 **casuist:** Don't **play the casuist** with me!
   a focus only on self-pleasure
   b act like a tough guy
   c make judgments about my conduct of duty
   d be stupid
4 **cyberpunk:** I like **cyberpunk**.
   a medicine that does not use drugs
   b one variety of science fiction
   c the art and science of eating
   d a society ruled by technical experts
5 **pussyfoot:** Let's not **pussyfoot around**.
   a criticize unreasonably
   b take care to avoid confrontation
   c attack indirectly
   d suddenly start

Check your answers. To arrive at an estimate of your knowledge of the 1,000 families in the 20,000 frequency band, multiply the number of items you answered correctly by 200. If you answered all five correctly, you are probably a highly proficient and highly educated speaker of English.

1 As you took the test, what kinds of knowledge informed your choices? For instance, did knowledge of word parts help you make guesses? Is something more than pure definitional knowledge being tested?
2 What other responses do you have to the test and its format? Can you imagine using it with a group of adolescent learners of English? Why or why not?
3 Some researchers have questioned estimating a learner's knowledge of entire 1,000-family-sized frequency bands on the basis of responses to only five questions per band. How serious an objection is this in your opinion? Does it call the usefulness of the VST into question?
4 To arrive at an estimate of your overall vocabulary size, take the entire VST. Several versions are available on the Victoria University of Wellington website, including eight bilingual versions (see Appendix). If you are a native speaker of one of these languages, take the version that allows you to answer in your L1. Why might the opportunity to answer in your L1 make the test a more sensitive measure?
5 If you are a native speaker of English or a very proficient non-native speaker, try taking both of the versions that go as far as the 20,000 frequency level. Were your results on the two versions similar? If not, how do you account for the discrepancy?

Answers: 1 a, 2 d, 3 d, 4 b, 5 b

The vocabulary size test from which the excerpt in Activity 4.1 was taken was used in New Zealand schools to investigate adolescent native speakers of English aged 13 through 17 years (Coxhead, Nation, & Sim, 2015). The 13-year-old learners were found to have an average vocabulary size of almost 11,000 words; the 17-year-olds averaged over 13,000 families. The research indicates that between the ages of 13 and 17, L1 English speakers learn about 600 new word families per year. These figures are useful baselines for comparisons to adolescent learners of English.

What does vocabulary size testing reveal about adolescent L2 learners of English and their language development? Much of the research that answers this question has been done in EFL contexts where school is the main source of exposure to English input. Spotlight Study 4.1 explores the vocabulary knowledge of teenaged learners in Denmark who had started studying English in primary school. The study illustrates how vocabulary size related to their performance on school tests of English.

Spotlight Study 4.1

In a study of 15- and 16-year-old Danish learners of English at the end of their ninth year of schooling, Stæhr (2008) investigated the relationship between the students' receptive vocabulary knowledge and their performance on tests of L2 English proficiency in three skill areas: reading, writing, and listening. To investigate their vocabulary size, he administered the Vocabulary Levels Test (VLT). This frequency-based test was originally devised by Nation in 1990 and improved by Schmitt, Schmitt, and Clapham in 2001 (see Appendix). Vocabulary size proved to be an important predictor of ability in all three skills. Of the three, the strongest connection was between scores on the vocabulary size test and performance on the reading comprehension measure. This was not surprising; many studies have identified a close association between measures of vocabulary knowledge and reading ability (Geva & Ramírez, 2015). The connection to comprehension of spoken language might be expected to be fairly weak given that the VLT assesses recognition of written words; however, the association between size scores and performance on the measure of listening comprehension proved to be substantial.

Stæhr's study shows the importance of learners' vocabulary knowledge in supporting their ability to do three different kinds of language tasks, but the actual numbers of VLT items answered correctly were found to be alarmingly low. The size testing indicated that over three quarters of the students had not mastered the 2,000 most frequent English word families—even after seven years of English instruction during their school years, which amounted to at least 570 hours spent in English classes. Words at this basic level include *curious, dozen, bitter, ancient,* and *social*.

This finding led Stæhr to examine performance at the 2,000-level more closely. He found that all students whose VLT scores indicated that they knew the full set of 2,000-level families scored well above average on all three of the skill tests. Although some of the students who did not know 2,000 families also scored above average on one or more of the tests, not knowing the 2,000 most frequent families was a strong predictor of below-average performance on the reading and writing measures. On the basis of these findings, Stæhr (2008, p. 139) concluded that 'the 2,000 vocabulary level is a crucial learning goal for low-level ESL learners', and he strongly advocates explicit classroom teaching of these words. His concern is justified given the importance of these families. As discussed in Chapter 1, coverage of the 2,000 most frequent English families is very high. These families account for about 85% of the words in written materials, 90% of unscripted spoken discourse (Nation, 2006), and 80% of the Middle School Content-Area Textbook Corpus (Greene & Coxhead, 2015).

In this study, size testing sheds light on the role of vocabulary in L2 reading, writing, and listening, but it also serves another important pedagogical purpose: the 2,000-level results send an unmistakable message about the word families these Danish students most need to study.

Other studies conducted in EFL settings where adolescent learners have limited exposure to English outside the classroom document similarly worrying low size results (Laufer, 2000), and rates of learning new words appear to be slow. In a study by Webb and Chang (2012), learners of English in Taiwan took vocabulary size tests every year over four years of high school and one year of university. At the end of the study, the researchers found that under half of the participants had mastery of the 1,000 most frequent English families and only 16% had achieved mastery of the 2,000 level. One of three tested groups had more hours of formal instruction than the other two. The average rate of growth for this group amounted to 430 new word families per year, but the figures were much smaller in the other two.

Milton (2009) examined the classroom exposure factor in a variety of foreign language learning contexts in classes where there was no special focus on vocabulary. The overview included primary, secondary, and older learners and two languages (French and English). The results were surprisingly consistent across the different settings: students gained an average of about four new word families per hour of classroom teaching.

Growth at this rate means that EFL learners in a program that offers two hours of English per week can be expected to learn about 300 new word families over the course of a 36-week school year. If we apply the rate to the Danish students in Spotlight Study 4.1, their 570 hours spent in English classes point to an overall average vocabulary size of about 2,300 families. Incidental vocabulary learning in classes where there is no systematic focus on high-frequency, mid-frequency, or academic words is hit or miss in character. That is, learners are likely to acquire words that are scattered all across the frequency zones and be left with incomplete knowledge of the families they most need to know. The findings reported by Stæhr (2008) and Webb and Chang (2012) bear this out.

Studies of minority-language adolescents in English-speaking countries paint a similar picture of deficits and low growth rates. For example, an investigation of 13-year-old middle school ELLs in a special language-support class in a California school, using Schmitt, Schmitt, and Clapham's VLT (2001 edition; see Appendix), showed that they knew just over half of the families on the part of the test that sampled vocabulary from the 3,000-frequency level and about a third of the families on the Academic Word List (AWL). Another study compared 13- and 14-year-old minority-language students who had studied in British schools for over ten years to L1 English speakers of the same age (Cameron, 2002). The native speakers outperformed the minority-language learners on all frequency levels tested, but with marked differences in knowledge of word families at the 3,000 and 5,000 frequency levels. Examples of 3,000-level words that the learners did not know are *peer*, *oblige*, and *climate*. Examples from the 5,000 level are *eagerness*, *pail*, *novelty*, and *paste* (p. 171). Most of these fit the description of Tier 2 vocabulary discussed in Chapter 3. They are words that are likely to be important for comprehending school texts, but they had not been learned through exposure to English at school or in the community.

Other kinds of measures have also been used to document the vocabulary development of adolescent learners of English. These include the PPVT and depth measures such as the Vocabulary Knowledge Scale (VKS) discussed in Chapter 1. Results are consistent with the findings of the size investigations discussed in this section. While some of the studies show that ELLs' vocabulary growth rates can match or even surpass those of native English speakers, ELLs in American schools are typically two to three years behind native English-speaking students of the same age in vocabulary knowledge, and the gap between the two groups is large (Mancilla-Martinez & Lesaux, 2011).

Support for Vocabulary Learning at School

In the previous section, we saw that L1-English speaking adolescents are estimated to recognize the meanings of well over 10,000 word families, while learners of English—both in contexts where English is a foreign language and in countries where it is the majority language—struggle with gaps at the most basic levels. The finding that many learners are not able to recognize all of the very frequent families in the 2,000 and 3,000 range even after many years of classroom study is particularly troubling; these deficits are likely to have a negative impact on all aspects of English language learning and make it difficult to meet academic goals at school.

It appears that the process of learning vocabulary incidentally through exposure to English input during the middle and high school years is simply not powerful enough to take adolescent learners beyond basic levels of English proficiency. At the rate of a few new words per hour of exposure, incidental acquisition of a vocabulary size on the order of the 8,000 families that are needed for unassisted comprehension of most English texts (Nation, 2006) becomes a difficult if not impossible proposition, requiring massive amounts of exposure. Studies of textbooks highlight the problem. Matsuoko and Hirsh (2010) investigated an ESL textbook written for upper-intermediate learners and found that 603 of the one thousand families at the 2,000 frequency level were used in the book. Of these, only 73 were recycled the ten or more times that research suggests is needed, on average, to support retention (Nation, 2013); only 15 AWL families occurred ten times or more. Martini (2012) analyzed an entire three-volume series of ESL textbooks designed for use by upper-secondary learners of English in Quebec, Canada. High-frequency words at the 1,000 and 2,000 frequency levels were well represented, but the potential for moving learners beyond these levels through exposure to the textbook materials was limited. Many but not all of the 3,000-level word families occurred at least once in the series; the majority occurred just once or twice. Only about a quarter of the 3,000-level families and less than a fifth of the 4,000-level families were recycled ten times or more.

How can educators tackle a learning task that is thousands of words large? One proposal is to greatly increase the amount of English input to which learners are exposed. Graded readers can provide opportunities to meet many high-frequency words repeatedly and are expressly designed to enable learners to make their way through a great deal of English input easily and enjoyably. They are written at different levels of difficulty and learners are encouraged to choose books at ever more challenging levels.

Programs of extensive reading using graded readers are often implemented in EFL settings where exposure to English outside of the classroom is limited. Nation (2008) recommends that learners complete 15–20 graded readers a year. Reading large amounts of simplified material is important in that it helps learners develop rapid word recognition skills. However, a limitation of simplified material is evident in the word *simplified*; most graded readers are not designed to move vocabulary learning beyond the 3,000 frequency level. A further problem for learning words beyond the 3,000 level incidentally through exposure is that they are not frequently used (and recycled) in more challenging reading materials either. Nation (2018) found that in 100,000-word stretches of five novels written for native speakers, the number of word families beyond the 3,000 level that were recycled five times or more was small, ranging from 180 to 431; very few occurred more than twelve times. This suggests that the amount of reading needed to learn thousands of mid-frequency words (the 4,000 to 8,000 most frequent families) incidentally through repeated reading encounters would be very great indeed—on the order of millions of words and dozens of novels—and well beyond what many ELLs can be expected to achieve.

An alternative to incidental acquisition is effective instruction that builds on learners' incidentally acquired vocabulary knowledge and prioritizes the words on the lists of the 1,000, 2,000, and 3,000 most frequent word families and the Middle School Vocabulary Lists (MSVL). To move beyond basic proficiency, adolescent learners of English need to know all of these words. They also need to work on acquiring mid-frequency vocabulary. Designing instruction to tackle these very large tasks clearly represents a great challenge. Later in this chapter, we will look at what schools and educational programs can do to make the learning of large numbers of words more systematic and efficient, and we will examine cases of effective vocabulary teaching. We will also see that the solution necessarily involves training learners to take on some of the responsibility of learning the vocabulary they most need to know for themselves.

Explanations for Growth

In Chapter 3, we saw that in low-income families, disadvantages such as impoverished language input in the home and limited access to literacy materials contribute to lower levels of vocabulary knowledge in young learners. These disadvantages can have a lasting impact. A study of Spanish-speaking ELLs in the United States by Kieffer (2012) showed that low levels of productive English vocabulary knowledge in early childhood were associated with poor reading ability many years later in eighth grade. In this section, the discussion of factors that can help and hinder adolescents in acquiring English vocabulary focuses mainly on learners' cognitive development. But this does not mean that the very real social problems many adolescent ELLs face should be overlooked. The factors that disadvantage the vocabulary acquisition of younger learners described in Chapter 3 affect older learners, too.

Cognition, Experience, Proficiency

Older learners often have the advantage of having more exposure to the second language than their younger peers. As might be expected, more exposure to English at school favors vocabulary development. Kohnert and Bates (2002) investigated the length of exposure factor for Spanish-speaking ELLs in the United States in a study that included learners as young as five years and as old as 20. All had begun learning English at about the same age in kindergarten or primary school. Performance on a test that asked them to listen to a spoken English word and to indicate whether it matched the image shown on a computer screen showed a pattern of improvement with age. Levels of accuracy increased up to the age of 14–16 years, at which point performance was near perfect; response times decreased with age through to adulthood.

Learners who begin acquiring a second language as adolescents have been found to learn vocabulary more quickly than those who start at a younger age. Evidence for this comes from a frequently cited study of English speakers who were learning Dutch while living in the Netherlands (Snow & Hoefnagel-Höhle, 1978). Whole families including children as young as three participated in the investigation. The researchers tracked the progress of the child, adolescent, and adult learners over the course of a year using a variety of measures including a version of the PPVT that had been developed for Dutch. Performance on almost all of the tests pointed to a distinct language learning advantage for the adolescents aged 12 to 15 years; of all the age groups, they made the fastest progress by far during the first few months. Over the course of the year of exposure to Dutch, the adolescents' scores on the PPVT continued to rise and were consistently well above those of the child learners. Research with L1 word learners confirms the adolescent advantage. In an investigation that brought together findings of 20 previous studies of learners in Grades 3 through 11, Swanborn and de Glopper (1999) found that older students were better able to learn new words incidentally from reading texts. Grade level proved to be a powerful predictor of the learning outcomes.

What makes adolescents such efficient vocabulary learners? The cognitive changes that children experience as they move into adolescence may offer an explanation. With more developed metalinguistic awareness, stronger memory capacity, and more advanced problem-solving skills in place, they are well equipped to take advantage of learning opportunities. The case of learning new words incidentally through reading or listening illustrates the importance of these cognitive assets; the information-processing perspective discussed in Chapter 2 sheds light on the process. First, learners need to be able to solve a logical puzzle. That is, they must use evidence—the meaning of the other words surrounding a new word, information available in the larger context, and morphological clues provided by the word itself—to make a guess about its meaning. Keeping the word in mind while forming hypotheses requires memory capacity. When partially learned words are met again in new contexts, the old hypotheses must be remembered, held in memory for testing against the new evidence, and refined.

Adolescent ELLs' knowledge of two languages may contribute to making them particularly good at this kind of cognitive work; research by Bialystok (2007) points to the benefits of bilingualism for the development of metalinguistic awareness. Kieffer and Lesaux (2012) characterize this bilingual advantage as follows:

> Although L2 learners may know fewer words in the second language than their L1 counterparts, they may know as much as or nearly as much as their counterparts about how words work, how they can be transformed morphologically, or about how context provides information about word meanings.
>
> (Kieffer & Lesaux, 2012, p. 353)

Other experiences that come with being older and spending more time at school also give adolescent ELLs a vocabulary-learning advantage. For example, adolescents are likely to have more reading experience and more practice in inferring the meanings of new words they meet than younger learners. With greater understanding of the world around them, they are likely to have a stronger knowledge base to support the making of informed guesses about the meanings of new words they encounter. The increases in proficiency that come with more exposure to the second language at school may make it easier to understand the spoken or written contexts surrounding new words and infer accurate meanings. Older learners may also have received more training in word learning strategies such as contextual guessing at school than younger learners.

So far in this discussion, we have noted factors that impact adolescents' incidental acquisition of words met over the course of exposure to the new language. What does research have to say about instructed vocabulary learning? Lawrence, Capotosto, Branum-Martin, White, and Snow (2012) investigated the effects of an intensive intervention that focused on teaching 11 words from the AWL to hundreds of sixth-, seventh-, and eighth-grade ELLs in the Boston area. The target vocabulary included *acquire, contrast, disproportionate, incentives,* and *relevant.* As the examples illustrate, the character of the words is abstract and scholarly. The study compared the learning outcomes of two groups of language-minority students: learners identified by schools and teachers as proficient in English, and learners who had been recently placed in school programs that offered support for their English language development and were therefore assumed to be less proficient. The more proficient learners made strong gains; tests administered a year later indicated that they had retained knowledge of the new words. By contrast, the less proficient ELLs did not appear to benefit from the teaching.

In explaining the results, the researchers suggest that the less proficient learners were unlikely to be independent readers and therefore probably had few opportunities to reinforce knowledge of the new academic words through meeting them in grade-level school texts. Such texts might not be available to learners in support programs; or, if available, they may be too difficult for them to process. Another explanation is the high cognitive demand the instruction placed on them. While the more proficient students could focus their energies on learning the new words and concepts, the less proficient students were engaged with the larger process of acquiring many other aspects of the new language while also trying to learn the new vocabulary. The results of the experiment illustrate the importance of adjusting vocabulary instruction to the proficiency level of the learners.

L2 Word Knowledge in Development

In this section, we examine what adolescent learners know and can do with words in their new language. We begin with a look at an important study that set out to explore different kinds of lexical ability in adolescent ELLs using 13 different measures. The goal was to determine what 'lexical ability' means. Would the testing show that the learners had 13 distinct kinds of vocabulary-related knowledge, or would some common themes emerge? The study and the answer to this intriguing question are detailed in Spotlight Study 4.2.

Spotlight Study 4.2

Kieffer and Lesaux (2012) investigated over 400 sixth-grade ELLs in seven middle schools in California. To assess various aspects of vocabulary knowledge, they administered 13 different tests. Some of the tests assessed recognition of word meanings. For example, students were asked to choose a correct synonym for *deceive* and other general English words in a multiple-choice format. Academic words from the AWL like *evidence* and *regulation* were also tested in this way. To assess depth of knowledge, learners were asked about words that do and do not 'go together'. For example, *effect* is closely associated with *cause*, *consequence*, and *result*, but less closely associated with *negative*, *policy*, and *people*. Another depth task asked them to demonstrate their understanding of the various meanings of polysemous words like *light*.

Other tests assessed the students' skills in guessing the meanings of rare words from context. Their awareness of word parts was also tested. For example, learners were asked to identify the headwords in affixed words like *complexity* and *possession*, and to recognize that among the non-words *tranter*, *tranting*, *trantious*, and *trantiful*, it is *tranter* that best completes 'The man is a great _____.'

The research showed that the adolescents' lexical ability boils down to three distinct types of word-related knowledge: vocabulary size, contextual sensitivity, and morphological awareness. Performance on the tests that assessed knowledge of word meanings (synonyms, word associations, polysemy) showed that these various ways of knowing meanings were all closely related to vocabulary size. This makes sense since being able to recognize the various meanings of *light* relies on recognition of the meanings of the other words in sentences like 'His shirt is light blue' and 'Light the fire in the fireplace' (Kieffer & Lesaux, 2012, p. 357). This finding indicates that instruction designed to increase learners' vocabulary size will also benefit their acquisition of deep vocabulary knowledge.

The finding that two other types of ability—contextual sensitivity and morphological awareness—were distinct from knowing word meanings also carries an important message for teaching. It tells us that in addition to teaching words, instruction should further develop learners' ability to use contextual clues to understand the meanings of new words and their awareness of word parts.

Kieffer and Lesaux's research is unusual in that it explored lexical ability in the same group of adolescents in so many different ways. Studies typically investigate just one or two types of knowledge, but their more comprehensive approach made it possible to identify converging themes in the learners' performance.

In addition to ELLs, Kieffer and Lesaux's (2012) study also investigated L1 English speakers. They outperformed the ELLs on the tests, but interestingly, the gap between the two groups was smaller on the measures of morphological awareness than on vocabulary breadth and contextual sensitivity. This suggests that although they have not yet caught up with their L1 classmates, the ELLs' metalinguistic knowledge of word parts may be particularly well developed, a finding that is consistent with the idea of a metalinguistic benefit for bilinguals. In Classroom Snapshot 4.1, a bilingual learner demonstrates his ability to use word-part knowledge to explain the meaning of *malevolent*.

Classroom Snapshot 4.1

Learners in a middle school in the southeastern United States were asked to talk about words (Pacheco & Goodwin, 2013). John speaks English and Spanish and has been identified as a struggling reader. Though the word is already familiar from a spelling list, his ability to identify the meaningful root *mal* is likely to make the word memorable.

John:	Malevolent.
Interviewer:	What do you think it means?
John:	A person that is really bad or is trying to do bad stuff.
Interviewer:	OK. How did you know that?
John:	Spelling word.
Interviewer:	Really? Anything else about the word?
John:	*Mal* [in Spanish], which means 'bad' or 'up to no good.'

Productive Use

What does research tell us about adolescents' use of the English vocabulary they know? Studies of their spoken productions are rare. One study of Dutch learners of English investigated the extent to which they resorted to using Dutch words in their speech (Poulisse & Bongaerts, 1994). For example, the word *ook* (too) appeared in the sentence 'I have *ook*, I have, uh, a brother, too'. As in this example, many of the speakers corrected themselves by adding the intended English word. The researchers compared the performance of university students, eleventh graders who had studied English for five years, and ninth graders who had studied English for three years. Results showed that all of the learners used Dutch words often in their speech, but there was a proficiency effect. Those who had studied English longer made fewer switches to Dutch.

Several studies have examined learners' writing. When essays produced by ESL learners in Grades 5 through 8 at schools in Texas were compared to essays on the same topics produced by L1 speakers of English, Reynolds

(2005) found that vocabulary use was less varied in the ESL learners' essays. But a study of lexical richness conducted with ESL learners aged 13 to 15 in Vancouver shows that, with well-designed vocabulary instruction, L2 writers can match or even surpass the productions of L1 English speakers. The research focused on vocabulary that occurred in a reading about the Titanic. The teacher read the text aloud and drew learners' attention to specific words that they were expected to use later in a writing task that asked them to imagine being on the sinking ship. Classroom Snapshot 4.2 illustrates the principled interactive approach to explaining the target vocabulary that was used in this study (Lee & Muncie, 2006, p. 302).

Classroom Snapshot 4.2

The teacher uses negotiation to explain or elicit meanings of the vocabulary. A definition is given, but there is also a contextual explanation and an illustration of the extended metaphorical meaning of *disaster*.

Teacher: What is *disaster*?
Students: Accident? Something bad?
Teacher: Yes, it's a very bad accident, but it also means the event causes a lot of suffering, hardship, sadness. Maybe many people die or lose their property. So, which is a better word: the Titanic sank and it was just an *accident*, or was it a *disaster*?
Students: Disaster.
Teacher: So, if a fire destroyed a whole neighborhood, what do you call that?
Students: Disaster.
Teacher: There's another meaning for *disaster*. For example, you invited twenty people to your birthday party, but there wasn't enough food and the music wasn't good. So everyone went home early. The party was a flop! It was a disaster.

The writing the students produced after listening to these explanations and rereading the passage showed that few of the new words were incorporated. However, after additional review and a task that involved writing, the ESL learners' accounts showed substantial use of the new vocabulary. The study illustrates the difficulty of moving new words into productive use, a challenge that has been noted by other researchers. This fact makes it even more impressive that, when the later written productions were compared to writing on the same topic produced by L1 English speakers at the same school, the L2 writing was found to be lexically richer, with a higher proportion of words beyond the basic 2,000 level than the L1 writing.

In Spotlight Study 3.2 (on page 88), we saw that young French-speaking learners' use of French and overly formal words borrowed from French decreased as their English proficiency developed (Horst & Collins, 2006). A study of EFL learners in Barcelona shows a similar trend in adolescent learners. Navés, Miralpeix, and Celaya (2005) examined English essays produced by Catalan-Spanish bilinguals in Grades 5 through 12. They looked for cases where the learners borrowed a word directly from Catalan or Spanish. An example is *para* (for) in 'The house is very big *para* my family'. They also looked for cases of lexical inventions where the learners adapted Spanish or Catalan words to look like English words. Examples are *scondite*, based on Spanish *escondite* (hide and seek), and *assignature*, based on Catalan *assignatura* and Spanish *asignatura* (school subject). The researchers found that reliance on these strategies decreased substantially among writers in the higher grades as amounts of classroom exposure to English increased. Counts showed that over a third of the fifth graders in the study had used words borrowed directly from Catalan or Spanish in their writing, but only a few of the twelfth-grade writers did this.

The study by Navés et al. (2005) raises the interesting question of how L1 speakers of Romance languages like Spanish and French can best exploit useful resemblances to Latinate vocabulary in English as they become more proficient. The finding that the older learners used fewer words taken directly from the L1 clearly represents a step towards more target-like English writing, as does the decrease in use of inventions that are not real English words. But inventing words based on Spanish or French will often lead learners to English words that are real, so this is not a strategy that developing learners should always suppress. The study found that the adolescent learners were increasingly able to avoid producing inventions that were too creative, but other research indicates that writers may be too cautious and reject the use of acceptable cognates (Granger, 1996; Lightbown & Libben, 1984). Granger's (1996) study of French-speaking university-level learners of English showed that in comparison to L1 English writers, the learners underused Latinate vocabulary in their writing and there was great overuse of basic English verbs like *think*, *take*, *put*, and *find*. Granger suggests that the learners avoided using French cognates because of their formal tone and the risk of making false-friend errors. We can conclude from this that teachers of English to Romance language speakers do well to encourage learners to notice and take advantage of cross-linguistic word resemblances, as these are often very helpful. Teachers can also raise awareness of the pitfalls for production, but emphasizing these too much may discourage learners' use of a very important asset: their first language.

Teaching the Vocabulary of School

What does effective teaching that targets the adolescent learner look like? In this section, we will explore ways of selecting suitable words and teaching them. Some themes will be familiar from the discussion of teaching younger learners in Chapter 3. Several strategies that enable adolescents to take their vocabulary learning beyond what is possible to achieve through classroom instruction alone will be emphasized.

Selecting Words

In selecting vocabulary to teach to adolescent learners, the guiding principle is need. Some secondary school students of English in EFL settings may aim to gain just enough proficiency to qualify for jobs that require a mid-level knowledge of English. Others may aspire to obtaining an advanced degree at an English-medium university. For many ELLs who are struggling to understand school reading materials in the low-income neighborhoods of American cities, graduating from high school may be the main goal. But in all of these contexts, students need to know most or all of the high-frequency vocabulary of English—the words on the lists of the 1,000, 2,000, and 3,000 most frequent families (Schmitt & Schmitt, 2014). Learners in schools also need to know the academic words found on the MSVL or the AWL. The task is large, but not as large as it sounds since there is overlap between some of these lists. Eventually, they will also need to know mid-frequency vocabulary (4,000 to 8,000 most frequent families). Size testing is a useful way of determining the vocabulary strengths and deficits of a particular group of learners.

In designing instruction to meet the needs of less advantaged ELLs and L1 English speakers in the United States, researchers agree that the first priority is the academic vocabulary that is frequently used in the learners' textbooks (Kelley, Lesaux, Kieffer, & Faller, 2010; Lawrence, White, & Snow, 2010). These are words such as *react*, *layer*, *structure*, and *affect* (all from the MSVL); in Chapter 3, such words were also referred to as Tier 2 vocabulary (see page 93). Teaching this general-purpose academic vocabulary is a good investment of class time because it supports learners as they try to comprehend their school reading. This vocabulary may be unfamiliar because it does not occur often in the language of everyday conversations. Neither is it given much attention in mainstream language arts classes in middle schools, where the focus is typically on unusual words (Kelley et al., 2010).

Many researchers argue that for vocabulary instruction to be effective, the number of selected words should be small. This is because learning all the meanings, morphological variants, and different uses of a new word is complex; students and teachers need to do a great deal of work on each word to ensure that words are learned beyond a superficial level. For example, the instructional units that Kelley et al. (2010) designed for sixth graders asked teachers to spend eight 45-minute lessons, six hours of class time in total, on teaching just eight or nine words. The results tell us that this was time well spent. By the end of the intervention, many students had learned dozens of new words and their reading comprehension had improved. But teaching a small number of words in great depth is clearly at odds with the goal of ensuring that learners know all of the many words on important lists such as the 570-family AWL or the BNC/COCA list of 3,000-level words. There is not enough time in the years of schooling available to adolescents to teach them all the words they need to know in depth. A goal for the rest of this chapter is to put forward ideas for instruction that resolve this contradiction.

Researchers recommend using interesting, age-appropriate expository texts as a starting point for designing deep vocabulary instruction for adolescents. Expository texts are recommended because they are more likely than narratives to contain useful academic words (Gardner, 2004, 2008). The next step is to select useful words in a chosen text. The VocabProfile tool on the Lextutor website (see Appendix) is useful for identifying words in a text that are found on the AWL or MSVL. As we saw in Chapter 3, the use of a reading passage is encouraged because the learners see how the words are used in a meaningful context, and the teacher can refer to the text to explain the words. But the use of texts is a hit-or-miss approach to ensuring that learners have opportunities to learn all of the hundreds of words on an important list such as the AWL. In the texts that might be used over the course of a school year, some AWL words might feature often, but others might occur only once or not at all. Ideas for giving systematic attention to all the words on an important frequency list are discussed at the end of this chapter.

Teaching Academic Vocabulary

As studies of effective vocabulary instruction of adolescent learners have shown, there needs to be a balance of two types of instruction: teaching new words and their meanings and teaching that focuses on strategies for detecting the meanings of words (Lesaux et al., 2014). We begin this section with a close look at the first side of this balance and consider how research-informed principles are implemented in the teaching of specific words.

Lawerence, White, and Snow (2010) designed a program of vocabulary instruction called Word Generation for middle school learners in low-income neighborhoods in Boston. Their investigation showed that the learners who participated in the 20-week program made vocabulary gains that normally take two years in regular classes. Both ELLs and at-risk L1 English speakers made lasting gains (Lawrence et al., 2012). On the first day of the sequence, the students met selected academic vocabulary words in the context of an interesting reading passage on a controversial topic such as renting a pet or withholding adoption information from parents. The teaching was cross-curricular. That is, the students first met the new words in an English class where they read the passage and discussed the words; the teacher provided simple definitions. Then in the days that followed, they encountered the words and the topic again repeatedly in mathematics, science, and social studies classes. For example, in social studies class, the students engaged in a debate on the topic. Finally, on the last day of the five-day intervention, the students wrote persuasive essays defending their position on the issue. Participation in this program proved to be beneficial for at-risk learners whose home language was English, but the effects were even larger for ELLs. Sample lessons are available on the Word Generation website (see Appendix). A program called ALIAS (Academic Language Instruction for All Students) developed by Lesaux, Kieffer, Kelley, and Harris (2014) for middle school learners in California has similar features.

There are a number of characteristics that explain the success of the learning sequence used in these programs. First, we see that the words are met many times in differing contexts. In Chapter 2, we discussed research showing that multiple opportunities for retrieval—as many as ten or more—contribute to the retention of new vocabulary. Meeting the words in different contexts is also consistent with the idea of elaborative learning. The learners are pushed to do the cognitive work of looking for similarities and differences in the ways the words are used in different subject areas. The debating and essay-writing tasks require production; these are tasks that require the learners to make personalized associations with the words. As discussed in Chapter 2, linking new words to previous knowledge and experience contributes to their integration into the mental lexicon. Learners use all four modalities in these elaborative activities: reading, writing, listening, and speaking.

Inferencing Skills

We noted above that effective programs of instruction also teach learners how to use strategies. The goal of this kind of instruction is for students to gain the cognitive tools they need to learn a large number of words independently. This is important because there is clearly a limit to the number of words that can be taught using the intensive and time-consuming 'rich' instruction outlined above. Successful interventions with adolescent ELLs have focused on three main strategies that can help students understand and remember new words: using morphological awareness skills, identifying and exploiting cognates, and inferring word meanings from context (Lawrence et al., 2012). All involve using clues in or around an unknown word to make a logical guess about its meaning. We will consider each of these more closely.

In their discussion of teaching learners to use word parts, Kieffer and Lesaux (2007) suggest modelling the process with learners when problem words are met in context. An example is the word *righteous* in the sentence 'Let's cheer for the *righteous* congressman who proposed changing the law'. The learners are encouraged to analyze the word for morphemes they recognize—both roots and suffixes. Once they have recognized the root *right* and the suffix *-eous*, which may be familiar from other words like *dangerous* and *mysterious*, they attempt to hypothesize a possible meaning. A final and very important step is to test the hypothesized meaning to see if it fits the overall meaning of the sentence. Developing learners' morphological awareness can also involve teaching the meanings of frequently used English affixes and useful Latin roots like *spect* (see) and *port* (carry).

Drawing on ELLs' knowledge of Spanish or other languages that share cognate vocabulary with English to arrive at the meaning of a word can also be modelled by the instructor, following a similar sequence of hypothesizing and confirming. The process can be facilitated by raising learners' awareness of patterns that make useful similarities more apparent. For example, students can be shown that the English words like *adjust* and *advance* use an *ad-* cluster that is not found in the Spanish cognate counterparts *ajustar* and *avance* (Moss, 1991). Other ideas for raising morphological and cognate awareness were outlined in Chapter 3.

Activity 4.2 is designed to replicate the experience of guessing the meanings of unknown words encountered while reading. The non-words embedded in the text occur at an approximate ratio of one unknown word in 20. This means that for readers who understand all the remaining real English words, the known-word density is 95%. As discussed in Chapter 2, research has shown that this level of coverage means that readers may find the text challenging but understandable. Coverage at the higher 98% level (one unknown word in 50) is more consistently associated with adequate comprehension and offers better support for guessing the meanings of words from context (Nation, 2013).

> **Activity 4.2**
> Read the passage and attempt to guess the meanings of the underlined non-words. Write a one-word meaning for each. As you work, monitor your process. What informs your guess in each case? The word itself, the use of the word in the sentence, or your understanding of the passage as a whole? If you have prior knowledge of the life of Leibniz, was this background knowledge helpful?
>
> The words used in the original version (Anton, 1980, pp. xxi–xxii) appear at the end of the passage.
>
> **Leibniz**
>
> Leibniz was born in Leipzig, Germany. His father, a professor of moral philosophy at the University of Leipzig, died when Leibniz was six years old. The 1) prolactic boy then gained 2) advelt to his father's library and began reading 3) emartically on a wide range of subjects, a habit that he maintained throughout his life. At age 15 he entered the University of Leipzig as a law student and by the age of 20 received a doctorate from the University at Altdorf. 4) Culberously, Leibniz followed 5) an aleand in law and international politics, serving as a 6) quelson to kings and princes.
>
> During his numerous foreign 7) latments, Leibniz came in contact with outstanding mathematicians and scientists who stimulated his interest in mathematics—most notably, the 8) cheltian Christian Huygens. In mathematics Leibniz was self-taught; he learned the subject by reading papers and 9) glises. As a result of this fragmented mathematical education, Leibniz often duplicated the work of others. This ultimately led to a raging conflict over who invented calculus, Leibniz or Newton. The argument over this question 10) seltranded the scientific circles of England and Europe. Most scientists on the continent supported Leibniz, while those in England supported Newton. The conflict was unfortunate, and both sides lost in the end.
>
> Words used in the original:
>
> 1 precocious
> 2 access
> 3 voraciously
> 4 subsequently
> 5 a career
> 6 counsel
> 7 missions
> 8 physicist
> 9 journals
> 10 engulfed
>
> (Nation, 1990, pp. 247–248)

Note that answers need not match the exact word used in the original. For instance, if your guess for *prolactic* was *clever* or *intelligent*, you succeeded in using the context to arrive at a partially correct approximation of the meaning.

Now consider the following questions and discuss with a colleague if possible:

1. Were you able to guess correctly most of the time? What clues did you miss?
2. Research indicates that most of the clues to meaning are found in the same sentence as the unknown word (Nation, 2013; van Zeeland, 2014). Was this your experience?
3. Was there enough information in the surrounding context to support good guesses in your view? In other words, is 95% coverage enough?
4. If a word you guessed does not match the meaning of the original word, think about the clues or information you used in choosing that word. Guesses for the last non-word (*seltranded*) are often off the mark. Frequently provided guesses are *separated* or *divided*. How do you explain these erroneous guesses?
5. How well does this activity replicate the experience of reading and guessing unknown words in a second language? How might a real L2 learner's experience differ?

L2 learners' ability and inability to guess meanings from context has attracted a great deal of research attention. New words are obviously met in attending to speech, but until recently, almost all of the work on guessing focused on inferring word meanings while reading. One question of interest is the adequacy of the information in the context surrounding unknown words for supporting good guesses of meanings. As the example of *seltranded* in Activity 4.2 illustrates, contexts can be under-informative or even misleading (Beck, McKeown, & McCaslin, 1983). Guesses meaning *divided* and *engulfed* are both supported by the sentence context in the activity. As Fukkink, Blok, and de Glopper (2001) point out, a single context can usually provide only partial information. Students should not be expected to give a dictionary-like definition of an unknown word after just one encounter. This reality points to the importance of meeting new vocabulary repeatedly in varied contexts so that there is a larger body of evidence for testing and refining hypotheses. Contextual guessing is a first step in a longer, incremental learning process.

Researchers also note the importance of being familiar with the concept of the new word. This issue is illustrated by the non-word *prolactic* at the beginning of the Leibniz passage in Activity 4.2. If the reader does not know of the word *precocious*, a term that describes children who seem older and more intelligent than would normally be expected, the reader will not succeed in guessing this meaning from context. Because adolescents tend to know more concepts, they are often more successful in guessing meanings from context than younger learners. Older learners have also been found to be more successful in guessing the meaning of abstract words like *dilemma* and *resolute* than younger learners (Fukkink, Blok, & de Glopper, 2001).

Another factor that favors older learners is the greater probability that they will have knowledge of the topic of the passage. If you have heard of Leibniz or have some familiarity with 17th-century European history, you may have had an easier time guessing the non-words in Activity 4.2 than a reader with no prior knowledge of this topic. Many studies confirm the importance of background knowledge in successful guessing. For this reason, teachers do well to choose materials on topics that are familiar and interesting to learners for practice in guessing meanings of unfamiliar words from context. When a topic is new to students, time spent exploring students' background knowledge of related topics and some key vocabulary can facilitate their comprehension of a reading passage. Finally, older learners are likely to know more L2 words than younger learners. Proficiency is a consistent predictor of successful guessing in reading studies, and van Zeeland's (2014) study of inferring word meanings from spoken input confirms the role of L2 vocabulary size in successful guessing in the listening mode.

Taken together, studies of L2 readers of varying ages and levels of proficiency show that, if partially correct guesses are taken into account, learners are successful in guessing word meanings from context roughly half of the time. In van Zeeland's (2014) study of adults guessing from listening, the success rate was lower—about one third. This may be explained at least in part by the finding that the learners had not noticed many of the target words in the spoken input.

In Classroom Snapshot 4.3, we see two secondary school learners of English in Denmark working together to guess the meaning of the word *insatiable* from a sentence context. The exchange, which was conducted in Danish, has been translated.

Classroom Snapshot 4.3

The context that was provided to the learners for the guessing-from-context task read as follows: '… a king called Chaka. He was a clever military leader with *insatiable* political ambitions. He won most of southeastern Africa and united …'

Student A:	*-able* means being able to—*insane*—*ins*
Student B:	I think it is a positive word—something with extremely great
Student A:	What does *sati* mean?
Student B:	*Satanic*. There is also a negation—it is something with *in-*—they couldn't be calmed down.
Student A:	Why do you think it is a negation?
Student B:	It usually is with *in-*. I mean the prefix.
Student A:	He sounds as if he is rather single-minded. *In-sa-ti,* okay—*in-* is something with *u-* [a prefix that often corresponds to English *in-* in Danish].
Student B:	This is a good word—oh, by the way, *sati* is related to *satisfy.*
Student A:	Yes. He has not yet been satisfied.

(Haastrup, 1991, p. 14)

The exchange illustrates the learners' ability to successfully exploit the morphological information available in *insatiable*. After some false starts, they use the prefix *in-* and the root *sati* along with the meaning of the larger context to arrive at a correct definition. However, the look of *insatiable* also prompts off-target guesses like *insane* and *satanic*. The tendency of L2 learners to arrive at wrong guesses that are explained by looking too closely at the form of the word while ignoring the larger sentence context is well documented (Bensoussan & Laufer, 1984; Nassaji, 2003). For this reason, Nation (2013) recommends that in modelling the process of guessing from context with a group of learners, the teacher does not begin with word-part analysis. Instead, learners can be directed to look at the words immediately surrounding the unknown word. This is where the clues needed to guess the word correctly are most often found. The next step is to look at the wider sentence or paragraph context. It may be useful to draw attention to the structure of the passage; for example, there may be a time sequence, cause-and-effect relationship, or other pattern that helps clarify the meaning. Then, a hypothesis can be ventured and checked to see if affixes and roots can offer any further help. Finally, the guess should be checked for its fit in the meaning of the sentence as a whole. Since guessing is an error-prone process, it is important to verify with the learners that they have arrived at a correct definition.

Concordancing

A word-inferencing activity that has received recent research attention is concordancing. Creating a concordancing activity involves using software to gather multiple examples of a word in use from a corpus. One example is the concordancing tool AntConc, which is available on Laurence Anthony's website (see Appendix). Concordancing tools are also available on the Lextutor website (see Appendix). The concordance lines in Activity 4.3 come from the Brown Corpus, a one-million-word corpus of press, journalism, and academic material gathered by Kučera and Francis (1967).

> **Activity 4.3**
>
> Examine the concordance lines in Figure 4.1 showing uses of *structure*, a word on the MSVL for science (Greene & Coxhead, 2015). What do they reveal about this word's meanings, part of speech, and collocations?
>
> ```
> s, the scientists who study the nature and STRUCTURE of the universe, to try to solve the great
> - and, in addition, employs an avant-garde STRUCTURE that particularly needs to be seen if comp
>  of having no means for inquiring into the STRUCTURE and meaning of this range of our experienc
> f our experience. There is no framework or STRUCTURE of thought with respect to which we can or
> reign countries to build a sound political STRUCTURE is more important than aiding them economi
> rops of our faith was to weaken the entire STRUCTURE. Doubts thus inculcated left me flounderin
> lies in institutions. Institutions require STRUCTURE, form, and definition, and these in turn e
> factors I mean those rooted in personality STRUCTURE. Some interfaith tensions are not occasion
> ring atoms of oxygen and make up the solid STRUCTURE of my finger bone. Since these electrons a
> y. Harmony, melody, counterpoint symphonic STRUCTURE are there; and as this music ebbs and flow
> universe. And so today when we examine the STRUCTURE of our knowledge of the atom and of the un
> rican dream, namely, the effort to build a STRUCTURE which would be something new in history an
> s later. On his first trip to the finished STRUCTURE he boasted that he had built a temple gran
>  house-building only, and had never seen a STRUCTURE of this nature; he certainly deserves not
>  distinction; that of being the first such STRUCTURE secured by force of arms in the war of the
> l on Jones and plead with him to spare the STRUCTURE; he reasoned and argued, pointing out that
> urpose. Centering around this historic old STRUCTURE, a group of public-spirited Barbour County
> ```
>
> **Figure 4.1** Concordance of 'structure' in the Brown Corpus (Kučera & Francis, 1967)
>
> 1 Did you identify more than one meaning of *structure*? What is the most frequent meaning? If you were defining this word for a group of learners, what would you say?
> 2 Which word occurs frequently after *structure* in the lines (five times)? Do you think this is a useful collocation for learners to know about?
> 3 Some educators feel that the format of concordance lines is unfriendly. If you were using the lines as an exercise with learners, would you adapt the format? How?
> 4 Are the wordings in the lines too difficult for L2 learners in your view? Do learners need to understand all of the words in the contexts to benefit from this exercise?

In a study of secondary school EFL learners in Vietnam, students made personalized electronic vocabulary notebooks using online resources (Karras, 2015). Some of the students used concordancing to search a corpus and find clear examples of words in use to add to their notebooks while others entered definitions from online dictionaries into their notebooks (Karras, 2015). The concordance-users outperformed the dictionary users on quizzes that featured questions like the example shown in Figure 4.2, where the word *advanced* can be used to appropriately fill all the blanks. This 'Which word fits all these?' format was also used by learners in research by Horst, Cobb, and Nicolae (2005) to review words studied in university ESL classes. Concordance exercises like the example in Figure 4.2, can be created by learners and teachers using the multi-concordance tool on the Lextutor website (see Appendix).

```
Question 1
[001] n. Paul led his guests into the dining-room. A waiter _____ towards their table, bent under the weight of an enor
[002] planet that promised so much? We are by far the most _____ race there has ever been, but we are terrified by the
[003] cario, Lindsay Davenport and Mary Joe Fernandez also _____ today, but ninth-seeded Gustavo Kuerten, 14th see
[004] tinuing education classes at Georgia Tech, Keller has _____ in his career and increased his income. For a growin
[005] assi had been a few hours earlier. William's victory _____ her to the fourth round in what is her first U.S. Open
[006] parts of the Sudan, the desert in just 15 years has _____ sixty miles. In just a few more years, more than half the
[007] e could you send me some more information about your _____ level courses, and an application form. How soon
[008] k you straight away, do you think that technology has _____ so far that soon, or within a few years, many people
```

Figure 4.2 Example concordance exercise

Concordancing is often used in exploring the meanings of words, but it is also used to raise learners' awareness of other linguistic features such as collocation patterns, grammar structures, and pragmatic chunks that recur in conversations. A comprehensive review of 64 studies of concordancing involving over 3,000 participants in schools and universities around the world showed that this approach results in powerful learning gains (Boulton & Cobb, 2017). One explanation for vocabulary gains achieved through concordancing is the cognitive effort involved in examining multiple examples of a word in context and identifying a shared meaning, or perhaps several related meanings. Learners engage in elaborative processing as they evaluate the contexts and attempt to arrive at generalizations. The concordance format makes learning through contextual guessing efficient. While learners may eventually meet a new word repeatedly over the course of exposure to large amounts of spoken or written language input, the encounters may be so widely dispersed that a guessed word and its partially learned meaning may not be remembered by the time the word is met again. By contrast, a concordance brings together multiple contextual examples in a short, richly informative format. Many learners are interested in using information and communication technology to search for answers to their language questions; concordancing offers a useful format for technology-based discovery learning.

Word Cards

The final strategy to discuss in this chapter is the use of word cards, a study technique that was once considered old-fashioned. A word card has a word on one side and information about its meaning on the other. The word card strategy is important because it helps teachers and learners address the challenge of mastering the very large numbers of words that middle school and secondary ELLs need to know. Teachers cannot give in-depth treatment to thousands of words in class, but they can make students aware of useful frequency-informed lists and encourage them to use cards to study dozens and even hundreds of word families.

There is theoretical support for learning from word cards. When learners make the cards, they engage in elaborative processing: writing the word on one side of the card focuses attention on spelling; adding a definition, translation, picture, or other information on the other engages the learner in thinking about meaning. Just making the cards has been shown to benefit learning (Nation, 2013), but the main theoretical argument for studying with word cards is their role in building strong form–meaning connections over the course of many retrievals. Every time the learner looks at a word on a card and tries to retrieve the meaning, or looks at the meaning and tries to remember the word and say it, the form–meaning connection is strengthened (Baddeley, 1990). Griffin and Harley (1996) report stronger learning effects for the second option, which involves producing the new word form. It must be acknowledged that word card study alone can hardly result in the full-fledged acquisition of all nine of the vocabulary knowledge components we examined in Activity 1.4 (see page 30), but the learning that can be achieved represents an important step in an incremental process. We can expect that words studied with cards will be noticed when they are met again later in a textbook or class discussion; and having knowledge of their meanings provides learners with a basis for making new associations and developing deeper knowledge.

What about the format of the cards? Nakata's (2008) investigation of secondary learners of English in Japan and their use of paper and computerized word cards did not identify learning differences between the two formats. Learning words from a list also proved to be effective. As for the information to include on the cards, pictures, examples of sentence contexts, collocates, grammar patterns, and other information can be included in addition to definitions or translations, though Nation (2013) suggests keeping the cards simple. There is evidence that L1 translations are more effective than L2 definitions (Laufer & Schmueli, 1997), probably because the meanings are more easily understood.

Much more important than the format is the way in which the cards are used. Massed repetition—reviewing the same word over and over and then moving on to the next card—is one of the least effective ways to study with word cards. Learning has been shown to be much more effective when a group of about 20 cards is reviewed quickly, reviewed again soon after, then reviewed again a day later, and so on. Spaced repetition following the principle of increasing time intervals has been shown to result in learning that will be retained for a long time (Baddeley, 1990; Nation, 2013).

Summary

This chapter outlined challenges facing adolescent ELLs when learning vocabulary. Their knowledge of English vocabulary often lags far behind that of their L1 English-speaking peers, and the learning task is large. Learners need to know thousands of high-frequency, academic, and mid-frequency word families, and the pace of learning vocabulary simply through exposure to English appears to be slow. However, adolescent learners have distinct assets that favor vocabulary learning. In comparison to younger learners, they have the advantage of more fully developed cognitive skills and may also benefit from having had more years of exposure to English. This chapter detailed the character of their developing vocabulary abilities. We saw that productions become richer over time and show less evidence of L1 influence. Programs of effective vocabulary instruction were described; notable features are the use of rich, elaborative techniques for teaching new words and an emphasis on learner autonomy. With so many words to know, enabling learners to learn words on their own is crucial. This means showing them how to determine the meanings of unfamiliar words for themselves by using context, word-part, and cognate strategies. Using online concordances also gives learners access to multiple examples of new words and allows not only practice in inferring meanings, but also exposure to other aspects of word knowledge. Finally, practice with word cards has also been found to be an effective and efficient way for learners to acquire knowledge of many new words on their own.

5

Vocabulary: What We Know Now

Preview

In this chapter, we return to the statements about vocabulary knowledge, learning goals, and teaching methods that you responded to in Activity 1.1. For each statement, I will provide a response based on the research that we have explored in this book. Before you read these responses, review your own ideas by returning to your answers to Activity 1.1.

> **Activity 5.1: Review your opinions**
> In Activity 1.1 (page 9), you indicated how strongly you agreed with some statements about teaching and learning second language vocabulary. Before you continue reading this chapter, go back and complete the questionnaire again. Compare the responses you gave then to those you would give now. Have your views about teaching and learning vocabulary been changed or confirmed by what you have read in the preceding chapters?

Reflecting on Ideas about Learning Second Language Vocabulary: Learning from Research

1 In classroom vocabulary teaching, any word that seems unfamiliar to a group of learners is worth explaining.

Words are not created equal. Some are very important to know and are worth explaining and reviewing in class, while others do not merit this amount of attention. Lists of the most frequent word families based on well-designed corpora of authentic English provide a principled basis for determining which vocabulary is worth spending precious class time on. Frequent words have a high value because they 'cover' more of the words in a stretch of speech or text. The importance of knowing the high-frequency vocabulary of general English—the words on the lists of the 1,000, 2,000, and 3,000 most frequent word families—cannot be overstated, and class time spent on teaching and learning them is time well spent. ELLs may know many high-frequency words, but research shows they often do not know them all. Academic words are also very important for ELLs to know and are worth teaching. The MSVL (Greene & Coxhead, 2015) and the AWL (Coxhead, 2000) are useful guides to frequent academic words.

Less frequent words merit less attention. Generally, teachers do well to not waste class time on explaining rare words. However, if a low-frequency word is essential to understanding a reading passage or participating in an activity, it will need to be explained. Another exception is low-frequency vocabulary that is domain-specific (for example, *chrysalis* and *pupa*). Explaining concepts such as these is an integral part of teaching school subjects.

2 Secondary school learners of English need to know roughly 5,000 word families to be able to succeed in their studies in mainstream classes in English-medium schools.

Secondary school ELLs need to be able to recognize the meanings of at least 5,000 word families. If students know 5,000 families and these include all of the high-frequency vocabulary of English, the academic words on the MSVL or AWL, and some mid-frequency words, levels of known-word coverage will be high. That is, the students will be familiar with a large proportion of the words used in textbooks and classroom discussions and this will be an asset in their study of school subjects. But it is not clear whether 5,000 is enough. Nation (2006) found that knowledge of at least 8,000 word families is needed to reach the level of coverage that is reliably associated with adequate comprehension of written language intended for adult native speakers. A study of 17-year-old native speakers in New Zealand (Coxhead et al., 2015) showed their average vocabulary size was about 13,000 families.

These figures set the bar high for teaching and learning. If the goal is knowledge of 13,000 word families by high school graduation, ELLs need to learn 1,000 families per year in 13 years of schooling. If all of these words were taught in class, over the course of five-day weeks and 30-week school years, instructors at all levels would need to teach six or seven families every school day. Since a family is made up of several members (*danger* includes *dangers, dangerous, dangerously, endanger,* and *endangered*), dozens of words would need to be taught every day. The teaching task is not as enormous as these figures suggest because learners acquire some L2 vocabulary knowledge incidentally. Nevertheless, the task is very large.

3 Children's first language knowledge has a positive impact on their second language vocabulary learning at school.

This statement is well supported by research. According to Cummins' (1979) interdependence hypothesis, children's first language ability plays a substantial role in supporting their development of second language proficiency at school. The relationship makes sense. Children who know a great deal of L1 vocabulary have a large store of named concepts in their mental lexicons available for linking to new L2 labels. ELLs' knowledge of two languages also appears to benefit their cognitive development; research by Bialystok (2007) shows that young bilinguals have particularly well developed metalinguistic awareness. Kieffer and Lesaux (2012) point out that even though L2 learners may not know as many L2 words as their L1 counterparts, the process of learning first language vocabulary means that they know a great deal about how words work. For instance, they may know how words can be transformed morphologically and how to use contextual information to infer the meanings of new words.

The connection between ELLs' L1 proficiency and their performance on tests of L2 vocabulary knowledge and measures of achievement at school constitutes an argument in favor of bilingual education programs that support learners' first language knowledge as they learn English.

4 Reading stories helps young children learn the academic vocabulary they need for success at school.

Academic vocabulary is relatively rare in stories; this is a limitation on their usefulness in teaching and learning the vocabulary of school. To acquire academic vocabulary, learners should be encouraged to read non-fiction. They are much more likely to meet the academic vocabulary they need for success at school in non-fiction than in fiction (Gardner, 2004, 2008). For the same reason, teachers should choose expository passages over stories as a basis for designing text-based academic word learning activities.

Although it provides limited support for learning academic words, reading stories is hardly to be discouraged. Reading storybooks aloud to young children exposes them to words they would not normally hear in conversations. Simple stories using familiar vocabulary are useful in helping beginning readers learn to decode words and practice sight vocabulary. Reading graded readers, fiction, or non-fiction can help ELLs learn high-frequency vocabulary and develop fluency. Nation (2008, 2013) emphasizes the importance of giving learners opportunities to read stories and other very easy reading materials that contain a minimal amount of new words. This allows learners to develop fluency, or automaticity, in using the vocabulary they know.

5 Once the teacher has explained a new word, the learner should be able to remember the word and use it.

In most cases, a single quick explanation of a new L2 word cannot be expected to result in retention of the form–meaning connection or the ability to use the word accurately. Cognate equivalents represent an exception: once Spanish speakers have understood that *nation* in English has the meaning of *nación* in Spanish, they will have little difficulty recognizing the meaning of *nation* when it is met again.

The idea that L2 vocabulary knowledge is acquired incrementally is well established. Receptive knowledge is built over the course of repeated opportunities to meet a new word and retrieve its meaning. Multiple opportunities to retrieve the form and produce it in speaking and writing are needed to advance productive knowledge. Once learners have receptive knowledge of new words, it may still be some time before they begin using them productively.

We have seen that knowledge of a word includes many different components. For example, full productive ability to use the word *expand* means knowing its morphological variants, relations to other words such as *contract* and *increase*, its collocations and uses in expressions, and more. Acquisition of this complex knowledge can be expected to proceed gradually. Classroom instruction that elaborates on various aspects of vocabulary knowledge can do a great deal to make new words memorable and promote learners' ability to use them productively, but teachers should not expect too much too soon. Acquiring deep knowledge of words takes time.

6 In teaching a new L2 word, the most important thing teachers can do is explain the meaning.

Learners clearly need to understand the meanings of new words. However, explaining meanings is often given too much emphasis at the outset. To illustrate, consider the following suggestion for introducing the lexical chunk *I'm sorry* to preschool or beginner-level ELLs. Note that it does not begin with explaining meaning (Calderón & Soto, 2017, p. 38).

Teacher: Say *I'm sorry* three times after I say it.
Students: *I'm sorry, I'm sorry, I'm sorry.*
Teacher: Now turn to your other buddy on the left, say *I'm sorry* three times, and pretend you are crying.
Students: [rubbing their eyes and pretending to cry] *I'm sorry, I'm sorry, I'm sorry!*

Instead of being told what *I'm sorry* means, the ELLs become familiar with the pronunciation through repetition. Attending to the spoken forms of words apart from attending to their meanings is consistent with the idea of avoiding cognitive overload. Barcroft's (2009) study of introducing new L2 words in a reading task highlighted this issue. He found that focusing learners' attention on the meanings detracted from their ability to remember the spellings of the new words.

After the repetition activity, Calderón and Soto (2017) suggest explaining *I'm sorry* briefly using a short definition and two simple examples of situations in which people feel sorry. The rationale for avoiding long, detailed explanations of meanings is the fact that ELLs have many concepts in place in their L1 lexicons; they already know what *accidents*, *forgetting homework*, and *feeling sorry* are. The challenge is to remember the new English word forms associated with the familiar concepts. The definitional meaning of a new word is just one of various knowledge aspects that teachers should address. Helping learners acquire knowledge of the form and use aspects of new words is important, too.

7 Once students know the base form of a new word, the meanings of the other family members will be obvious.

L1 English speakers and ELLs develop awareness of word roots and parts during the primary school years, and their skills in recognizing them increase throughout high school. But we should not assume that knowing the meaning of a word guarantees all of its family members will be easily understood. Recognizing words may be challenging in cases where adding an affix substantially alters the root word (*divide/division*, *clarify/clarification*). This is an argument for working with affixes like *un-* and *-ness* that do not involve a spelling (and pronunciation) change to the word that present more complexity; these affixes are also useful to know because they occur frequently (Nation, 2013). Bauer and Nation (1993) provide a helpful scheme that orders the affixes of English according to their complexity and frequency.

Rich, elaborative instruction of new words should raise learners' awareness of their morphological variants. For example, if *environment* has been selected for teaching and the passage that the students are working with also has *environmentally* in it, the teacher should draw students' attention to the two forms. Research shows that learning to use affixed words productively is particularly challenging for learners of English. That is, learners who see the connection between *environment* and *environmentally* in a reading passage might not be able to produce the word *environmentalist* on their own. This tells us that teaching should involve learners in both recognizing and producing affixed forms of words.

8 Understanding the basic meaning of 'pick' helps learners of English understand expressions like 'pick up a language' and 'pick on someone'.

For ELLs, knowing the meaning of *pick* is probably not very helpful in understanding the meanings of *pick up* and *pick on*. A well-known feature of lexical chunks is their lack of transparency; that is, knowing the meanings of the component words is often not helpful in understanding the meaning of the whole. By contrast, the component words in *baseball glove* and *bicycle helmet* offer much more transparent clues to meaning.

Vocabulary teaching that involves learners in the elaborative processing of new words draws their attention to the other words that can 'go with' a particular word. This is straightforward in cases of transparent chunks such as *bicycle helmet*; the teacher can work with learners in thinking of other kinds of *helmets* or other words that go with *bicycle*. The situation of the polysemous word *pick* and the collocates *up* and *on* is more complicated. One of the meanings of *pick* is 'to take a flower, fruit, or vegetable from where it is growing'. It may be possible to relate this meaning to the idea of *pick up a language*, but the use of *up* in the combination is harder to explain. This is an argument for teaching *pick up* as if it were a single word with its own meaning of 'to learn something without formal training'.

Chunking is a frequent phenomenon, but a particular chunk may be very infrequent. When selecting chunks for instructional attention, teachers do well to focus on those that are frequent and likely to be met again. Thus, we might question whether spending a lot of class time on *pick up a language* is a wise investment.

9 When nine of the words in a ten-word sentence are understood, the meaning of the remaining unknown word can be easily guessed from the others.

When one unknown word is surrounded by nine known words, guessing the meaning of the unknown word successfully will probably be difficult. Research consistently shows that a much higher level of support is needed. In the case of written English, when 98% of the words are familiar—amounting to just one unfamiliar word in 50—L2 readers should be able to read a text, understand it adequately, and guess the meanings of the unfamiliar words. Hiebert (2012) recommends known-word coverage at the 98–99% level for primary-school L1 readers. Van Zeeland and Schmitt (2013) determined that a slightly lower level of coverage—95%—is needed to adequately understand informal spoken narratives. Too often, materials used with learners contain too many difficult words. The vocabulary level of a passage can be checked using VocabProfile on the Lextutor website or using AntWordProfiler, available on Laurence Anthony's website (see Appendix). The output shows the proportions of high-frequency words in the entered text.

Successful guessing of word meanings from context is not guaranteed. Even with high levels of known-word support, guesses may be incorrect because the surrounding language does not provide enough information.

10 Learning new words 'naturally' through reading or hearing them in use is an effective way to learn vocabulary.

Preschool children learn the words of their first language through exposure to spoken input in the home, and incidental acquisition accounts for most of the thousands of words that native speakers eventually acquire over the course of a lifetime. Research shows that ELLs also acquire new word knowledge through reading and listening to comprehensible input. Given these realities, we can conclude that incidental vocabulary acquisition is an effective process.

However, it is not very efficient. The rate of incidental vocabulary learning is slow; studies show that reading an entire book might result in the acquisition of just a few new words. ELLs need to know many words and they need to know them right away. Intentional study of words has been consistently shown to lead to greater word learning gains and better retention. For this reason, classroom instruction that develops ELLs' vocabulary knowledge is important in addressing their needs at school. But we need not reject one process in favor of the other. Incidental and intentional learning support each other. Knowledge of words studied in class is reinforced later when the words are met in a movie or a textbook. When learners have some previous knowledge of words through exposure, this enriches their classroom study of the words.

11 Teachers should encourage their students to study lists of words by practicing with word cards.

Reviewing words and definitions with word cards is a useful way of learning new vocabulary. Opportunities for multiple retrievals are important in building new form–meaning connections. Word cards are ideal for this kind of practice. Since it may not be feasible for classroom instruction to address all of the word families on important lists, such as the MSVL (Greene & Coxhead, 2015), word cards offer a way for learners to study large numbers of these words on their own. Research by Elgort (2011) shows that word knowledge gained through studying word cards is not as static and limited as might be expected. She found that the new vocabulary learned with cards became well integrated into the L2 learners' mental lexicons and could be accessed rapidly. There are now many apps available for word-card study; these include Quizlet, Memrise, Anki, VTrain, and Lextutor flashcard builder (see Appendix).

12 Adolescents learn L2 vocabulary more quickly than younger learners.

Adolescent ELLs are more efficient vocabulary learners than their younger brothers and sisters. Strong evidence for the adolescent advantage comes from a study of English speakers who were learning Dutch while living in the Netherlands. The study tracked the progress of the child, adolescent, and adult learners and found a distinct language learning advantage for the adolescents aged 12 to 15 years; of all the age groups, they made the fastest progress by far (Snow & Hoefnagel-Höhle, 1978).

Cognitive changes that children experience as they move into adolescence may explain why adolescents learn vocabulary more quickly. With more developed metalinguistic awareness, stronger memory capacity, and more advanced problem-solving skills in place, adolescents are well equipped to take advantage of word learning opportunities. They are also likely to have more reading experience and more practice in inferring the meanings of new words than younger learners. With greater understanding of the world around them, they have a stronger knowledge base to support the making of informed guesses about the meanings of new words. Because they have spent more time at school, older learners may also have received more training in word learning strategies than younger learners.

13 Teachers should point out cross-language word resemblances even though the L1 and L2 meanings do not always match up perfectly.

The availability of cognates offers a potentially powerful vocabulary advantage for learners who know a language that shares cognate vocabulary with English. In the majority of cases, cognates are 'true friends'; that is, the resemblance to the L1 cognate can be trusted to be a helpful clue to the meaning of the English word. For this reason, teachers should encourage learners to use the cognate strategy. It is estimated that Spanish and English share over 10,000 cognates. But learners need to be able to see the cross-language connections in order for them to be useful. Not all connections are as easy to recognize as in the English–Spanish pairs *prediction/predicción* and *result/resultado*. Learners may not immediately see the connection between English *survive* and Spanish *sobrevivir*, for example. If teachers know the learners' L1, they can point out spelling patterns that can make recognition easier.

Sometimes, cross-language resemblances are misleading. As we have seen in Chapter 3, an English word may have a close formal resemblance to a word in another language that has a very different meaning. However, the problem of 'false friends' should not be overestimated. Making cognate connections may lead to occasional errors, but it remains an effective strategy most of the time.

14 Teachers should train learners in techniques for guessing the meanings of new words.

Effective vocabulary instruction should include showing learners how to use strategies for detecting word meaning. Since only a portion of the many words learners need to know can be taught and reviewed in class, empowering ELLs with strategies for advancing their vocabulary learning on their own is critical. Guessing the meaning is not the same thing as learning and remembering the new word, but it is an important step in the learning process. One way of identifying the meaning of an unfamiliar word is the cognate strategy discussed above. We have also discussed the strategy of examining a word to see if word parts—prefixes, suffixes, and the root—can offer clues to meaning. Another important strategy is using the words surrounding an unfamiliar word to guess its meaning. None of these strategies is foolproof, and incorrect guesses are common. For this reason, strategy training should also include a reminder to verify guesses by consulting a dictionary or asking the teacher.

Conclusion

Learning the vocabulary of a new language is an enormous challenge. In this book, there have been many references to 'the thousands of words learners of English need to know', and lists containing hundreds and even thousands of words have been mentioned often. Teachers may feel a heavy burden of responsibility. There is indeed a very large vocabulary teaching job to do, but with the responsibility comes the potential to bring about positive change in people's lives. Knowing vocabulary empowers language learners; it is relevant to every school subject. We have seen research evidence that vocabulary knowledge can be a very important determinant, or even the main determinant, in learners' success in mastering academic content.

Learning words impacts their trajectory at school and may eventually shape the course of their lives. I hope that this book has provided insights into the learning process and practical solutions that will be useful to teachers as they undertake this important work. Finally, we must acknowledge the work that students do. It is they who take on the ultimate challenge of learning the words of a new language.

Suggestions for Further Reading

Baker, S., Lesaux, N., Jayanthi, M., Dimino, J., Proctor, C. P., Morris, J., Gersten, R., Haymond, K., Kieffer, M. J., Linan-Thompson, S., & Newman-Gonchar, R. (2014). *Teaching academic content and literacy to English learners in elementary and middle school (NCEE 2014–4012)*. Washington, DC: National Center for Education Evaluation and Regional Assistance (NCEE), Institute of Education Sciences, U.S. Department of Education. Retrieved from: https://ies.ed.gov/ncee/wwc/Docs/PracticeGuide/english_learners_pg_040114.pdf

> A practical guide to supporting primary and middle school learners' acquisition of academic language. Four literacy-related teaching recommendations are made, all strongly supported by research. The first of these reads: 'Teach a set of academic vocabulary words intensively across several days using a variety of instructional activities' (p. 6). Many specific suggestions for implementing the recommendation are given in the form of activity ideas, example texts, and samples of teacher talk. The guide targets learning in primary and middle school classrooms where there is a mix of ELLs and students whose first language is English.

Calderón, M., & Soto, I. (2017). *Academic language mastery: Vocabulary in context*. Thousand Oaks, CA: Corwin.

> Though the cover information tells us that this book is meant for teachers of both ELLs and L1 English students, the authors' keen awareness of the needs of ELLs is evident. The focus is on learning academic and domain-specific vocabulary. The book offers many principled teaching suggestions following a pre-, during-, and post-reading sequence. The activity ideas target learners of various levels from kindergarten all the way through high school. Suggestions are given for adjusting the activities to suit older or younger learners as needed. The authors are clear and direct—about what teachers should

do, and also what they should definitely *not* do. A strength of this book is its emphasis on learning large numbers of words.

Gardner, D. (2013). *Exploring vocabulary: Language in action*. Abington, Oxon: Routledge.

Following the practice-to-theory structure of the 'Exploring' series, Gardner begins with a close look at corpus-based frequency lists, showing why they are important and how they can be used to address ELLs' vocabulary needs. The book features engaging tasks designed to guide readers in making useful discoveries; these make what might be an intimidating topic come alive. Learners' needs, as delineated by the corpus methodologies described at the outset, form the basis for the theory-informed approaches to teaching vocabulary discussed in the second part of the book. Most of the classroom activities provided in this section target older, more advanced learners. The appendices (nine!) are a rich resource for information about frequently used words, lemmas, compounds, and more.

Geva, E., & Ramírez, G. (2015). *Focus on reading*. Oxford: Oxford University Press.

Because reading ability and vocabulary knowledge are so closely intertwined, this book dedicated to reading has a great deal to offer to readers interested in the vocabulary development of young classroom learners. Like other volumes in the Key Concepts series, the focus is on ELLs. Geva and Ramírez bring valuable insights from reading research to topics such as learning to decode words in early reading and the role of academic word knowledge in successful reading in high school. They include many practical suggestions for teaching vocabulary.

Greene, J. W., & Coxhead, A. (2015). *Academic vocabulary for middle school students: Research-based lists and strategies for key content areas*. Baltimore: Brookes.

The authors describe how they collected the Middle School Content-Area Textbook Corpus, a compilation of 109 textbooks used by middle school learners in the United States, and analyzed the corpus to create the Middle School Vocabulary Lists. These are lists of academic word families that occur frequently in five subject areas: 1) English grammar and writing, 2) health, 3) mathematics, 4) science, 5) social studies and history. This book is the primary source for the actual lists, but there is much more on offer. Greene and Coxhead provide guidelines for using the word lists with middle school learners and there is a large chapter devoted to classroom activities.

Kelley, J. G., Lesaux, N. K., Kieffer, M. J., & Faller, S. E., (2010). Effective academic vocabulary instruction in the urban middle school. *The Reading Teacher*, 64(1), 5–14.

> This article provides a valuable set of guidelines and activity suggestions for teachers of middle school learners, based on the authors' experience of implementing an intensive vocabulary intervention in urban schools where about 70% of the learners were minority language students. The focus is on teaching small sets of high-utility academic words following a rich instruction approach that includes reading, speaking, and writing activities. To cope with the many words that cannot be treated in this in-depth way, the experimental instruction also emphasizes strategy training. The article is written in an approachable style, with many concrete guidelines for teaching and a number of interesting student and teacher responses.

Scott, J. A., Skobell, B. J., & Wells, J. (2016). *The word-conscious classroom: Building the vocabulary readers and writers need*. Santa Cruz, CA: Text Project.

> This book is devoted to showing teachers how to make the classroom an 'enticing vocabulary-learning environment for children' (p. 5). The authors seek to remove the anxiety teachers may feel about teaching vocabulary and to foster a love of words—in the belief that teachers' enthusiasm for words will be communicated to their students. Teachers are encouraged to read with their students and have them note favorite 'powerful words' that are then added to class word banks called 'Gifts of Words'. The early emphasis on reading stories moves to reading longer books, with many ideas for consolidating word knowledge through writing poetry, memoirs, and short stories. Reading and writing in the academic mode are discussed, but the main focus is on classroom uses of children's literature. The target audience is teachers of primary and middle school learners in mainstream classes that include ELLs.

Webb, S., & Nation, P. (2017). *How vocabulary is learned*. Oxford: Oxford University Press.

> This recent addition to the Oxford Handbooks series is a state-of-the-art resource for teachers of secondary or university-level learners in ESL or EFL contexts. Frequency-based approaches to determining the words

learners need to know and the conditions that support vocabulary learning are described clearly with reference to current research and theory. Much of the book is devoted to explaining research-informed principles that underpin effective vocabulary learning and applying these to the design of classroom activities, strategy instruction, and even entire courses. Chapters make use of an engaging question and answer format.

Thornbury, S. (2002). *How to teach vocabulary.* Harlow, UK: Pearson Education Limited.

Although this book was written well over a decade ago, it remains popular with instructors in university training programs for teachers of English as a second language. Experienced teachers will also profit from reading it. Thornbury has an engaging style and explains complex concepts in an accessible manner. Principles derived from research are supported by many examples and the volume is richly illustrated. Topics range widely from using dictionaries to playing games and testing vocabulary. Suitable for teachers of learners of English of all ages in both ESL and EFL settings.

Zimmerman, C. B. (2009). *Word knowledge: A vocabulary teacher's handbook.* Oxford: Oxford University Press.

Zimmerman draws on the knowledge framework by Nation (1990, 2013) that we examined in Chapter 1 to explore ways of working with learners in acquiring knowledge of meanings, collocations, word parts, grammatical features, and register. Each chapter focuses on one of these components; after the knowledge aspect is examined closely, teaching guidelines and sample activities are provided. There is also a useful chapter on strategy training. Suitable for teachers of secondary and university students; suggestions can also be adapted for use with younger learners.

Appendix

Academic Vocabulary List (AVL)
www.academicvocabulary.info

Academic Word List (AWL)
www.victoria.ac.nz/lals/resources/academicwordlist

Anki
https://apps.ankiweb.net

AntConc
www.laurenceanthony.net/software.html

AntWordProfiler
www.laurenceanthony.net/software/antwordprofiler

BNC/COCA headword lists
https://www.victoria.ac.nz/lals/about/staff/paul-nation#vocab-lists

British National Corpus (BNC)
www.natcorp.ox.ac.uk

Corpus of Contemporary American English (COCA)
http://corpus.byu.edu/coca

French–English cognates activities
http://doe.concordia.ca/alert/teaching-materials/cognates-unit.html

General Service List
www.victoria.ac.nz/lals/about/staff/paul-nation#vocab-lists

Lextutor concordancers
www.lextutor.ca/conc

Lextutor flashcard builder
www.lextutor.ca/cgi-bin/flash

Lextutor multi-concordance tool
www.lextutor.ca/conc/multi

Memrise
www.memrise.com

Middle School Vocabulary Lists (MSVL)
www.lextutor.ca/vp/eng

Picture Vocabulary Size Test (PVST)
www.laurenceanthony.net/software/pvst

Quizlet
https://quizlet.com/en-gb

Threshold word list
www.ealta.eu.org/resources.htm
www.lextutor.ca/vp/comp (see 'CEFR 2' list)

VocabProfile
http://www.lextutor.ca/vp

Vocabulary Levels Test (VLT)
www.lextutor.ca/tests (2001 edition)
www.edu.uwo.ca/faculty-profiles/stuart-webb.html (updated 2017 edition)

Vocabulary Size Test (VST)
www.lextutor.ca/tests
https://www.victoria.ac.nz/lals/about/staff/paul-nation#vocab-lists

VTrain
www.vtrain.net/down3.htm

V_YesNo
www.lognostics.co.uk/tools

Waystage word list
www.ealta.eu.org/resources.htm
www.lextutor.ca/vp/comp (see 'CEFR 1' list)

Word Generation
http://wordgen.serpmedia.org

Glossary

academic vocabulary: Words that occur frequently across a range of school subjects (for example, *major*, *investigate*, and *isolate*). Academic vocabulary is typically used to explain concepts at school and university and is less likely to occur in everyday conversations. Another term used for this concept is Tier 2 words.

Academic Word List (AWL): The AWL is made up of 570 academic word families that occur frequently in university reading across a variety of subjects. It is based on a 3.5-million-word corpus of university textbooks representing 14 different subject areas. Developed by Coxhead (2000).

affixed word: A word that has a prefix or a suffix or both. *Impolitely* is an example of an affixed word (*im* + *polite* + *ly*).

alphabetic system: A way of representing written language, following the principle of letter–sound correspondence. Letters represent speech sounds. English, French, Turkish, and Spanish are examples of languages with an alphabetic system.

automaticity: The ability to do something quickly and with little cognitive effort. Repetition and practice contribute to automaticity. In vocabulary learning, automaticity is reflected in the ability to recognize or produce a word rapidly without conscious effort.

basic interpersonal communicative skills (BICS): The informal, conversational language used in everyday communication in social situations. L2 learners typically acquire BICS more quickly than *CALP*.

behaviorism: A psychological theory which states that language and other skills are learned through the establishment of habits. According to this view, habit formation (or learning) occurs when learners imitate and reproduce words or phrases they hear in the language around them and are positively reinforced for doing so.

chunk: A sequence of words that commonly occur together (for example, *teddy bear*, *catch a cold*, and *be fed up with something*). Other terms used to refer to this concept are *collocation*, *formulaic sequence*, and *multi-word unit*.

cognate: A word that has a formal resemblance to a word in another language. A Spanish–English example is *familia/family*. The meanings of cognates are often (but not always) similar across languages. The term *cognate* is also used to describe languages that have a shared history. For example, Spanish and French are cognate languages.

cognate awareness: A learner's ability to recognize formal resemblances between words across languages; for example, to see that English *family* resembles Spanish *familia*.

cognitive academic language proficiency (CALP): The type of language ability needed to function well in school settings. Academic language is more formal, often more decontextualized, and more challenging for L2 learners to acquire than *BICS*.

collocation: A sequence of words that commonly occur together. An example is *strong coffee*. It is possible to say *powerful coffee*, but it is considered unconventional. Other terms used to refer to co-occurring words are *chunk*, *formulaic sequence*, and *multi-word unit*.

communicative competence: The ability to use language in a variety of settings, taking into account relationships between speakers and differences in situations. The term is sometimes used to refer to the ability to convey messages effectively even though language use is not entirely accurate.

compound word: A combination of two or more words that function as a single unit of meaning. English compounds may be separate words (*teddy bear*), hyphenated (*merry-go-round*), or joined (*cellphone*).

comprehensible input: A term used to refer to language that a learner can understand. The language may be comprehensible because many of the words and structures are known. Other factors that may contribute to comprehensibility are clues to meaning in the immediate context or the learner's familiarity with the topic.

concordance: A list of the examples of a single word or phrase found in a text or corpus, usually gathered electronically.

connectionist theory: A theory of knowledge (including language) as a complex system of units that become interconnected in the mind as they are encountered together. The more often the units are encountered together, the stronger the associations become.

corpus (plural: **corpora**): A collection of texts that is designed to be representative of a type of language. For example, a child speech corpus contains many transcribed samples of oral language produced by children. The collection is searchable electronically.

coverage: The proportion of the words in a continuous stretch of language that is accounted for by a list of words or the vocabulary size of a learner, usually expressed as a percentage. When a learner has known-word coverage at around the 98% level, the material is likely to be understood adequately.

declarative knowledge: Knowledge that we have and know we have. For example, an English-speaking learner of Spanish might have knowledge of a word that can be stated as: 'I know that *casa* in Spanish means *house* in English.' Some information-processing perspectives on language acquisition hypothesize that learning begins with declarative knowledge. This contrasts with *procedural knowledge*.

decode: To read words by applying letter–sound correspondence rules. This is commonly known as 'sounding out' words.

derivation: A change made to a headword by adding a prefix or suffix; for example, the formation of *happiness* and *unhappy* from the root word *happy*. Derivation usually changes the part of speech and/or the meaning of the word; for example, adding the suffix *-ness* to the adjective *happy* results in the noun *happiness*. Adding the prefix *un-* to *happy* results in a word with the opposite meaning: *unhappy*.

discourse: A stretch of spoken or written language that is larger than a single sentence.

domain-specific vocabulary: Words that occur in a specific subject area and are less frequently used outside that area; for example, *chrysalis* and *pupa* are words likely to be used in a biology lesson. Other terms used for this concept are technical, specialized, and Tier 3 words.

elaborative processing: Making a new word memorable by establishing mental pathways for retrieving the word. For example, the learner can relate the word to a personal experience, create an association to an image, analyze the word parts, or make a connection to a first language cognate.

expository: This kind of language is informative. It is typically used to explain or describe something in writing. An expository text is more likely than a story or conversation to include the use of academic vocabulary.

first language (L1): The language first learned. Other terms for this concept are *mother tongue* or *native language*. Some children learn more than one language from birth and can be said to have more than one 'first language'.

formulaic sequence: A sequence of words that commonly occur together; for example, *teddy bear*, *catch a cold*, and *be fed up with something*. Other terms used to refer to this concept are *chunk*, *collocation*, and *multiword unit*.

genre: A type of language that has a distinct style. Academic language used in textbooks is an example; another example is fiction.

graded readers: Books written in simple language designed for use by language learners, graded by difficulty level. They can be simplified versions of classics or original books. Graded readers provide repeated encounters with high-frequency vocabulary and the opportunity to develop reading fluency.

headword: The basic form of a word as it appears at the beginning of a dictionary entry, for example *guess*. Adding prefixes or suffixes to a headword results in inflections (*guessed, guessing*) or derivations (*unguessed, guessable*).

incidental learning hypothesis: According to this hypothesis put forward by Nagy, Herman, and Anderson (1985), children's vocabulary growth during their school years is the result of large amounts of reading. They argue that the thousands of words that adults eventually come to know could not possibly all have been taught at school; therefore, people must be 'picking up' new word knowledge from their reading.

incidental vocabulary learning: The learning of vocabulary as the by-product of another activity such as reading a story or doing another task that is not explicitly geared to vocabulary learning. It stands in contrast to *intentional vocabulary learning*, where the learner makes a deliberate effort to commit new words to memory.

inflection: A change to a headword made by adding a grammatical ending. For example, *carries*, *carried*, and *carrying* are formed from the headword *carry*. Inflectional endings do not usually change the part of speech or the meaning of the word.

information-processing: A psychological theory based on the idea that learners' cognitive resources are limited and that they cannot pay attention to everything at the same time. When applied to learning vocabulary, the theory predicts that making a connection between a word form and its meaning will initially require attention, but with repeated retrievals it will become automatic, leaving more attention available to focus on something else.

integrated form-focused instruction: This refers to instruction that draws attention to a word (or other linguistic feature) in the midst of communicative classroom interaction. The teacher may quickly provide a definition or other information, correct a learner's misuse of the word, or simply highlight it.

intentional vocabulary learning: The learning of vocabulary where the learner makes a deliberate effort to commit new words to memory (for example, word card practice). It stands in contrast to *incidental vocabulary learning* in which the learner may 'pick up' some vocabulary knowledge while engaged in an activity that is not focused on learning words.

interdependence hypothesis: A proposal that a child's first language knowledge and skills are instrumental in the development of second language proficiency.

keyword mnemonic: A powerful elaborative technique that makes use of imagery to link a new word's meaning to its spoken form. It involves thinking of a familiar word that sounds like the new word and then creating a mental image that connects the two. If the new word is French *navet* (turnip) and the English-speaking learner of French thinks it sounds something like *navy* in English, imagining a navy blue turnip may help the learner remember *navet*.

learner corpus (plural: **corpora**): A collection of written or spoken language produced by second language learners that is stored in a searchable electronic format.

lemma: A unit of counting words. A lemma is made up of a headword (for example, the verb *expect*) and its inflected forms (*expects, expected*, and *expecting*). A lemma is a smaller unit than a *word family*, which includes derived forms (such as *expectation*).

lexical frequency profiler: A computerized tool that reveals frequency information about the words in an entered text, such as the frequency level of each word and the lexical coverage of the text for learners with different vocabulary sizes.

lexical richness: The extent to which a learner's speech or writing exhibits the use of unusual, varied, or 'sophisticated' vocabulary.

lexicon: The store of words in an individual's mind.

loanwords: Words that have been borrowed from another language, often with little modification. Examples of Spanish loanwords in English are *amigo, taco,* and *burro*.

low-frequency: This term describes vocabulary that is not common in spoken and written language. Schmitt and Schmitt (2012) define low-frequency vocabulary as word families that are at the 9,000 most frequent level or beyond (i.e. even less frequent).

metalinguistic awareness: The ability to reflect on language and manipulate it. For example, being able to define a word or say what sounds are found in it.

Middle School Vocabulary Lists (MSVL): The lists are made up of AWL and other academic word families that occur frequently in an 18-million-word corpus of 109 textbooks used by middle school students (Grades 6, 7, and 8) in the United States. There are sub-lists of roughly 400 families each for five subjects: 1) English grammar and writing, 2) health, 3) mathematics, 4) science, 5) social studies and history.

mid-frequency: This term describes vocabulary found on the lists of the 4,000 through 8,000 most frequent families. These words represent an important learning target for advanced learners.

morphological awareness: The ability to recognize spoken and written word parts and use them as clues to meaning. For example, a child with morphological awareness knows that a *chanter* is probably a person who chants, even though the word *chant* may be unfamiliar. It is an aspect of *metalinguistic awareness*.

morphology: This term pertains to the roots, prefixes, and suffixes that make up a word. For example, the word *readjustments* consists of the root form *adjust*, prefix *re-*, suffix *-ment*, and the plural marker *-s*.

multi-word unit: A sequence of words that commonly occur together (for example, *teddy bear, catch a cold,* and *be fed up with something*. Other terms used to refer to this concept are *chunk, collocation,* and *formulaic sequence.*

noticing: The process of becoming aware that something in the language input is unfamiliar. For example, a learner may realize that the meaning of a particular word is not known. The learner may also notice the spelling, pronunciation, grammar or other aspect of a word. It has been proposed by Schmidt (2001) that language learners can only learn that which they have first noticed.

orthography: The writing system of a language. Orthography is concerned with matters of spelling and the extent to which letters correspond to sounds.

phonological awareness: The knowledge that spoken words are made up of sounds and syllables. If a child is asked to remove the *b* at the beginning of *bring* and they can say that the resulting word is *ring*, this is an indicator of phonological awareness. It is an aspect of *metalinguistic awareness*.

phonological memory: The capacity to hold a small amount of information in mind for a short time. This mental attribute is often measured using tasks that require the test taker to attend to and repeat non-words such as *kabbit* and *consamponita* that are presented orally.

polysemous: Having different but related meaning senses. For example, the word *wood* can refer to a material made from trees or to a forested area.

pragmatics: Language knowledge that involves an understanding of the social context in which it is appropriate to use a word (or other language feature). Using *please* to ask a stranger for help is an example. Using the chunk *you know* to make a conversation partner feel included is another.

procedural knowledge: Knowledge that underlies fluent or automatic performance. It is contrasted with *declarative knowledge*.

productive knowledge: The ability to use a word in its spoken or written form to express an intended meaning. The acquisition of productive knowledge of words tends to occur after the words have been acquired receptively. Also known as active knowledge.

receptive knowledge: The ability to understand the meanings of words when they are heard or met in reading. Receptive knowledge is easier to gain than productive knowledge, and people know more words receptively than productively. Also known as passive or recognition knowledge.

register: A variety of language that has unique characteristics. For example, the casual register used with friends may make use of slang. By contrast, the register used in professional settings is more formal.

retrieval: The process of searching for the form or meaning of a word. Receptive retrieval occurs when a learner sees or hears a word and recalls its meaning. Retrieval is productive when the learner has a concept in mind and recalls the word form needed to express the meaning.

rich instruction: A series of activities designed to develop comprehensive knowledge of a word. It develops knowledge of multiple aspects such as written form, spoken form, meaning, morphology, collocation, and grammatical features.

second language (L2): In this book, the term refers to any language other than the first language learned. Thus, it may actually refer to a learner's third or fourth language.

semantic: Related to meaning or distinctions between meanings.

sequential bilingual: A learner who learns one language first and then another. Sequential bilingualism stands in contrast to simultaneous bilingualism, in which both languages are learned at the same time.

sight word: A high-frequency word that cannot be read by relying on decoding because of inconsistent letter–sound relationships; for example, *should*, *through*, and *know*. With practice, sight words are recognized automatically.

simultaneous bilingual: A learner who learns two languages at the same time. Simultaneous bilingualism stands in contrast to sequential bilingualism, in which one language is learned before another.

socioeconomic status (SES): The economic and social position of individuals or groups in relation to others in a society. SES levels are based on income, education, and occupation.

transfer-appropriate processing (TAP): This hypothesis is based on the observation that when we learn something new, we also internalize some of the circumstances and thinking processes that were present when we learned it. For this reason, newly learned information tends to be easier to retrieve in conditions that resemble the original learning situation.

type of processing–resource allocation (TOPRA): This hypothesis predicts that increased use of cognitive resources to work on one kind of learning reduces the resources available for doing another kind of processing (Barcroft, 2002).

usage-based theory: In this theoretical approach, language acquisition can be explained by learners' ability to perceive patterns in the language to which they are exposed. See also *connectionist theory*.

vocabulary depth: Knowledge of a word that goes beyond the ability to make a basic form–meaning connection; for example, knowing the different meanings the word can have, its morphological variants, or its use in expressions.

vocabulary size: The number of word families that learners can recognize and associate with a simple definition.

word family: A unit of counting words. Word families are made up of a headword (for example, *expect*), its inflected forms (*expects, expected, expecting*), and derived forms (*expectant, expectation, expectantly, unexpected*, etc.).

word map: A graphic organizer that shows the words and phrases associated with a target word. Also known as word web and semantic web.

Zipf's law: A frequency patterning of words in natural language use. George Zipf found that if we rank words according to their use, there is a pattern such that the most frequent word is twice as frequent as the next most frequent word, approximately three times as frequent as the next most frequent word, and so on. This patterning means that there are relatively few high-frequency words and many more low-frequency words. It also means that the chances of meeting many words that are not high-frequency repeatedly in a single novel or textbook are very low.

References

Agustín-Llach, M. P., & Canga Alonso, A. (2014). Vocabulary growth in young CLIL and traditional EFL learners: evidence from research and implications for education, *International Journal of Applied Linguistics*, 26(2), 211–227.

Aitchison, J. (1994). *Words in the mind: An introduction to the mental lexicon*. Oxford: Blackwell.

Anderson, J. R. (1990). *Cognitive psychology and its implications* (3rd ed.). New York: Freeman.

Anderson, R. C., Wilson, P. T., & Fielding, L. G. (1988). Growth in reading and how children spend their time outside of school. *Reading Research Quarterly*, 23, 285–303.

Anthony, L., & Nation, I. S. P. (2017). Picture vocabulary size test (1.0.0). Retrieved from http://www.laurenceanthony.net/software/pvst/

Anton, H. (1980). *Calculus*. New York: Wiley.

August, D., Carlo, M., Dressler, C., & Snow, C. (2005). The critical role of vocabulary development for English language learners. *Learning Disabilities Research & Practice*, 20(1), 50–57.

Baddeley, A. (1990). *Human memory*. London: Lawrence Earlbaum Associates.

Baker, S., Lesaux, N., Jayanthi, M., Dimino, J., Proctor, C. P., Morris, J., Gersten, R., Haymond, K., Kieffer, M. J., Linan-Thompson, S., & Newman-Gonchar, R. (2014). *Teaching academic content and literacy to English learners in elementary and middle school (NCEE 2014-4012)*. Washington, DC: National Center for Education Evaluation and Regional Assistance (NCEE), Institute of Education Sciences, U.S. Department of Education. Retrieved from the NCEE website: http://ies.ed.gov/ncee/wwc/publications_reviews.aspx.

Barcroft, J. (2002). Semantic and structural elaboration in L2 lexical acquisition. *Language Learning*, 52, 323–363.

Barcroft, J. (2009). Effects of synonym generation on incidental and intentional vocabulary learning during reading. *TESOL Quarterly*, 43(1), 79–103.

Bauer, L., & Nation, I. S. P. (1993). Word families. *International Journal of Lexicography*, 6(4), 253–279.

Baumann, J. F., Font, G., Edwards, E. C., & Boland, E. (2005). Strategies for teaching middle-grade students to use word-part and context clues to expand reading vocabulary. In E. H. Hiebert & M. L. Kamil (Eds.), *Teaching and learning vocabulary: Bringing research to practice* (pp. 179–205). Mahwah, NJ: Lawrence Erlbaum Associates.

Beck, I. L., McKeown, M. G., & Kucan, L. (2005). Choosing words to teach. In E. H. Hiebert & M. L. Kamil (Eds.), *Teaching and learning vocabulary: Bringing research to practice* (pp. 207–222). Mahwah, NJ: Lawrence Erlbaum Associates.

Beck, I. L., McKeown, M. G., & McCaslin, E. S. (1983). Vocabulary development: All contexts are not created equal. *Elementary School Journal, 83,* 177–181.

Beck, I., McKeown, M., & Omanson, R. (1987). The effects and uses of diverse vocabulary instructional techniques. In M. McKeown & M. Curtis (Eds.), *The nature of vocabulary acquisition* (pp. 147–163). Hillsdale, NJ: Erlbaum.

Bensoussan, M., & Laufer, B. (1984). Lexical guessing in context in EFL reading comprehension. *Journal of Research in Reading, 7,* 15–32.

Bialystok, E. (2007). Cognitive effects of bilingualism: How linguistic experience leads to cognitive change. *International Journal of Bilingual Education and Bilingualism, 10,* 210–223.

Biemiller, A. (2003). Vocabulary needed if children are to read well. *Reading Psychology, 24,* 323–335.

Biemiller, A. (2005). Size and sequence in vocabulary development: Implications for choosing words for primary grade vocabulary instruction. In E. H. Hiebert & M. L. Kamil (Eds.), *Teaching and learning vocabulary: Bringing research to practice* (pp. 223–242). Mahweh, NJ: Lawrence Erlbaum Associates.

Biemiller, A. (2010). *Words worth teaching: Closing the vocabulary gap.* Columbus, OH: McGraw-Hill.

Biemiller, A., & Boote, C. (2006). An effective method for building meaning vocabulary in primary grades. *Journal of Educational Psychology, 98*(1), 44–62.

Biemiller, A., & Slonim, N. (2001). Estimating root word vocabulary growth in normative and advantaged populations: Evidence for a common sequence of vocabulary acquisition. *Journal of Educational Psychology, 93*(3), 498–520.

Bloom, L., Hood, L., & Lightbown, P. M. (1974). *Imitation in language development: If, when, and why. Cognitive Psychology, 6,* 380–420.

Bolton, K., & Graddol, D. (2012). English in China today: The current popularity of English in China is unprecedented, and has been fuelled by the recent political and social development of Chinese society. *English Today, 28*(3), 3–9. doi:10.1017/S0266078412000223

Boulton, A., & Cobb, T. (2017). Corpus use in language learning: A meta-analysis. *Language Learning, 65*(2), 1–46.

Calderón, M., August, D., Slavin, R., Duran, D., Madden, N., & Cheung, A. (2005). Bringing words to life in classrooms with English-language learners. In E. H. Hiebert & M. L. Kamil (Eds.), *Teaching and learning vocabulary: Bringing research to practice* (pp. 115–136). Mahwah, NJ: Lawrence Erlbaum Associates.

Calderón, M., & Soto, I. (2017). *Academic language mastery: Vocabulary in context.* Thousand Oaks, CA: Corwin.

Cameron, L. (2002). Measuring vocabulary size in English as an additional language. *Language Teaching Research, 6*(2), 145–173.

Carlo, M. S., August, D., McLaughlin, B., Snow, C. E., Dressler, C., Lippman, D. N., Lively, T. J., & White, C. E. (2004). Closing the gap: Addressing the vocabulary needs for English language learners in bilingual and mainstream classrooms. *Reading Research Quarterly, 39*(2), 188–215. doi:10.1598/RRQ.39.2.3.

Chall, J. S. (1996). *Stages of reading development* (2nd ed.). Fort Worth: Harcourt Brace.

Chall, J. S., & Jacobs, V. A. (2003). The classic study on poor children's fourth-grade slump. *American Educator*, 27(1), 14–15, 44.

Chen, X., Ramírez, G., Luo, Y. C., Geva, E., & Ku, Y. (2012). Comparing vocabulary development in Spanish- and Chinese-speaking ELLs: The effects of metalinguistic and sociocultural factors. *Reading and Writing*, 25(8), 1991–2020.

Chomsky, N. (1959). Review of *Verbal behavior* by B. F. Skinner. *Language*, 35(1), 26–58.

Clark, E. V. (1993). *The lexicon in acquisition.* Cambridge: Cambridge University Press.

Cobb, T. (2007). Computing the vocabulary demands of L2 reading. *Language Learning & Technology*, 11(3), 38–63.

Cobb, T., & Horst, M. (2011). Does *Word Coach* coach words? *CALICO Journal*, 28(3), 639–661.

Cobo-Lewis, A., Pearson, B. Z., Eilers, R. E., & Umbel, V. C. (2002). Effects of bilingualism and bilingual education on oral and written English skills: A multifactor study of standardized test outcomes. In D. K. Oller & R. E. Eilers (Eds.), *Language and Literacy in Bilingual Children.* Clevedon, UK: Multilingual Matters.

Corson, D. (1995). *Using English words.* Dordrecht: Kluwer Academic Publishers.

Coxhead, A. (2000). A new academic word list. *TESOL Quarterly*, 34, 213–238.

Coxhead, A., Nation, P., & Sim, D. (2015). Vocabulary size and native speaker secondary school students. *New Zealand Journal of Educational Studies*, 50, 121–135. DOI: 10.1007/s40841-015-0002-3.

Cummins, J. (1979). Cognitive/academic language proficiency, linguistic interdependence, the optimum age question and some other matters. *Working Papers on Bilingualism*, 19, 121–129.

Cummins, J. (2000). *Language, power and pedagogy: Bilingual children in the crossfire.* Clevedon: Multilingual Matters.

Cummins, J. (2008). BICS and CALP: Empirical and theoretical status of the distinction. In B. Street. & N. H. Hornberger, (Eds.), *Encyclopedia of Language and Education, Volume 2: Literacy* (2nd ed.) (pp. 71–83). New York: Springer Science + Business Media LLC.

Cunningham, A. E. (2005). Vocabulary growth through independent reading and reading aloud to children. In E. H. Hiebert & M. L. Kamil (Eds.), *Teaching and learning vocabulary* (pp. 45–68). Mahwah, NJ: Lawrence Erlbaum Associates.

DeKeyser, R. (1998). Beyond focus on form: Cognitive perspectives on learning and practicing second language grammar. In C. J. Doughty & J. Williams (Eds.), *Focus on form in classroom second language acquisition* (pp. 42–63). Cambridge: Cambridge University Press.

Dockrell, J. E., Braisby, N., & Best, R. M. (2007). Children's acquisition of science terms: Simple exposure is insufficient. *Learning and Instruction*, 17, 577–594.

Dudley-Marling, C., & Lucas, K. (2009). Pathologizing the language and culture of poor Children. *Language Arts*, 86(5), 362–370.

Dunn, M., & Dunn, L. M. (1959). *Peabody Picture Vocabulary Test.* Circle Pines, MN: American Guidance Service.

Durgunoğlu, A. Y., Nagy, W. E., & Hancin-Bhatt, B. J. (1993). Cross-language transfer of phonological awareness. *Journal of Educational Psychology, 85*(3). 453–465.

Dutro, S., & Moran, C. (2003). Rethinking English language instruction: An architectural approach. In G. Garcia (Ed.), *English learners: Reaching the highest level of English literacy* (pp. 227–258). Newark, DE: International Reading Association.

Elgort, I. (2011). Deliberate learning and vocabulary acquisition in a second language. *Language Learning, 61*(2), 367–413.

Ellis, N. C., Römer, U., & O'Donnel, M. B. (2016). *Usage-based approaches to language acquisition and processing: Cognitive and corpus investigations of construction grammar.* Hoboken, NJ: Wiley-Blackwell.

Ellis, N., & Wulff, S. (2015). Usage-based approaches in second language acquisition. In B. VanPatten & J. Williams (Eds.), *Theories in second language acquisition: An introduction* (2nd ed.) (pp. 75–93). London/New York: Routledge.

Elley, W. B. (1989). Vocabulary acquisition from listening to stories. *Reading Research Quarterly, 24,* 174–187.

Eurostat. (2017). *Foreign language learning statistics.* Retrieved from: http://ec.europa.eu/eurostat/statistics-explained/index.php/Foreign_language_learning_statistics

Farnia, F., & Geva, E. (2011). Cognitive correlates of vocabulary growth in English language learners. *Applied Psycholinguistics 32,* 711–738.

Favreau, M., & Segalowitz, N. S. (1983). Automatic and controlled processes in the first- and second-language reading of fluent bilinguals. *Memory & Cognition, 11,* 565–574. doi:10.3758/BF03198281

Fukkink, R., Blok, H., & de Glopper, K. (2001). Deriving word meaning from written context: A multicomponential skill. *Language Learning, 51*(3), 477–496.

Gardner, D. (2004). Vocabulary input through extensive reading: A comparison of words found in children's narrative and expository reading materials. *Applied Linguistics, 25*(1), 1–37.

Gardner, D. (2008). Vocabulary recycling in children's authentic reading materials: a corpus-based investigation of narrow reading. *Reading in a Foreign Language, 20*(1) 92–122.

Gardner, D. (2013). *Exploring vocabulary: Language in action.* Abington, Oxon: Routledge.

Gardner, D., & Davies, M. (2014). A new academic vocabulary list. *Applied Linguistics, 35*(3), 305–327.

Geva, E., & Ramírez, G. (2015). *Focus on reading.* Oxford: Oxford University Press.

Godfroid, A., Housen, A., & Boers, F. (2010). A procedure for testing the Noticing Hypothesis in the context of vocabulary acquisition. In M. Pütz & L. Sicola (Eds.), *Inside the learner's mind: Cognitvie processing and second language acquisition* (pp. 69–197). Amsterdam/Philadelphia: John Benjamins.

Goldberg, H., Paradis, J., & Crago, M. (2008). Lexical acquisition over time in minority first language children learning English as a second language. *Applied Psycholinguistics 29,* 41–65.

Granger, S. (1996). Romance words in English: from history to pedagogy. *KVHAA Konforenser, 36,* 105–121.

Greene, J. W. (2008). *Academic vocabulary and formulaic language in middle school content area textbooks.* (Unpublished doctoral dissertation). Georgia State University, Atlanta.

Greene, J. W., & Coxhead, A. (2015). *Academic vocabulary for middle school students: Research-based lists and strategies for key content areas*. Baltimore: Brookes.

Griffin, G. F., & Harley, T. A. (1996). List learning of second language vocabulary. *Applied Psycholinguistics, 17*, 443–460.

Haastrup, K. (1991). *Lexical inferencing procedures, or, talking about words: Receptive procedures in foreign language learning with special reference to English*. Tübingen: Gunter Narr Verlag.

Hancin-Bhatt, B., & Nagy, W. (1994). Lexical transfer and morphological development. *Applied Psycholinguistics, 15*, 289–310.

Harley, B. (1992). Patterns of second language development in French immersion. *French Language Studies, 2*, 159–183.

Hart, B., & Risley, T. R. (1995). *Meaningful differences in the everyday experience of young American children*. Baltimore: Paul H. Brookes Publishing Co.

Hart, B., & Risley, T. R. (2003). The early catastrophe. The 30 million word gap by age 3. *American Educator, 22*, 4–9.

Hasselgren, A. (1994). Lexical teddy bears and advanced learners: A study into the ways Norwegian students cope with English vocabulary. *International Journal of Applied Linguistics, 4*(2), 237–258.

Hatch, E., & Brown, C. (1995). *Vocabulary, semantics, and language education*. New York: Cambridge University Press.

Hedgecock, J. S., & Ferris, D. (2018). *Teaching readers of English: Students, texts and contexts* (2nd ed.). New York: Routledge.

Henriksen, B. (1999). Three dimensions of vocabulary development. *Studies in Second Language Acquisition, 21*, 303–317.

Hiebert, F. (2012). Core vocabulary: The foundation for successful reading of complex text. *Text Project*. Retrieved from http://textproject.org/professionaldevelopment/text-matters/

Horst, M. (2009). Developing definitional vocabulary knowledge and lexical access speed through extensive reading. In Z. H. Han & N. J. Anderson (Eds.), *L2 reading research and instruction: Crossing the boundaries* (pp. 40–64). Ann Arbor: University of Michigan Press.

Horst, M. (2013). Mainstreaming second language vocabulary acquisition. *Canadian Journal of Applied Linguistics, 16*, 171–188.

Horst, M., Cobb, T., & Meara, P. M. (1998). Beyond *A Clockwork Orange*; Acquiring second language vocabulary through reading. *Reading in a Foreign Language, 11*, 207–223.

Horst, M., Cobb, T., & Nicolae, I. (2005). Expanding academic vocabulary with an online collaborative word bank. *Language Learning and Technology, 9*, 90–110.

Horst, M., & Collins, L. (2006). From 'faible' to strong: How does their vocabulary grow? *Canadian Modern Language Review, 63*, 83–106.

Horst, M., & Meara, P. M. (1999). Test of a model for predicting second language lexical growth through reading. *Canadian Modern Language Review, 56*, 308–328.

Horst, M., White, J., & Bell, P. (2010). First and second language knowledge in the language classroom. *International Journal of Bilingualism. 14*(3), 331–349.

Hulstijn, J. H. (2001). Intentional and incidental vocabulary learning: A reappraisal of rehearsal, elaboration and automaticity. In P. Robinson (Ed.), *Cognition and second language instruction* (pp. 258–287). Cambridge: Cambridge University Press.

Hulstijn, J. H., & Laufer, B. (2001). Some empirical evidence for the Involvement Load Hypothesis in vocabulary acquisition. *Language Learning, 51,* 539–558.

Hyland, K., & Tse, P. (2007). Is there an 'academic vocabulary'? *TESOL Quarterly, 41*(2), 235–253.

Joe, A. (1998). What effects do text-based tasks promoting generation have on incidental vocabulary acquisition, *Applied Linguistics, 19,* 357–377.

Joe, A., Nation, P., & Newton, J. (1996). Vocabulary learning and speaking activities. *English Teaching Forum, 34*(1), 2–7.

Karras, J. N. (2015). The effects of data-driven learning upon vocabulary acquisition for secondary international school students in Vietnam. *ReCALL, 82,* 166–186.

Kelley, J. G., Lesaux, N. K., Kieffer, M. J., & Faller, S. E. (2010). Effective academic vocabulary instruction in the urban middle school. *The Reading Teacher, 64*(1), 5–14.

Kieffer, M. J. (2012). Early oral language and later reading development in Spanish-speaking English language learners: Evidence from a nine-year longitudinal study. *Journal of Applied Developmental Psychology, 33,* 146–157

Kieffer, M. J., & Lesaux, N. K. (2007). Breaking down words to build meaning: Morphology, vocabulary, and reading comprehension in the urban classroom. *The Reading Teacher, 61*(2), 134–144.

Kohnert, K., & Bates, E. (2002). Balancing bilinguals II: Lexical comprehension and cognitive processing in children learning Spanish and English. *Journal of Speech, Language, and Hearing Research, 45,* 347–359.

Krashen, S. (1982). *Principles and practice in second language acquisition.* Oxford: Pergamon.

Kučera, H., & Francis, W. N. (1967). *Computational analysis of present-day American English.* Providence: Brown University Press.

Lam, K., Chen, X., Geva, E., Luo, Y. C., & Li, H. (2012). The role of morphological awareness in reading achievement among young Chinese-speaking English language learners: a longitudinal study, *Reading and Writing, 25,* 1847–1872.

Laufer, B. (1997). What's in a word that makes it hard or easy: some intralexical factors that affect the learning of words. In N. Schmitt & M. McCarthy (Eds.), *Vocabulary: Description, acquisition and pedagogy* (pp. 139–155). Cambridge: Cambridge University Press.

Laufer, B. (2000). Task effect on instructed vocabulary learning: The hypothesis of 'involvement'. *Selected Papers from AILA '99 Tokyo* (pp. 47–62). Tokyo, Japan: Waseda University Press.

Laufer, B., & Shmueli, K. (1997). Memorizing new words: Does teaching have anything to do with it? *RELC Journal, 28,* 89–108.

Laufer, B., & Waldman, T. (2011). Verb-noun collocations in second language writing: A corpus analysis of learners' English. *Language Learning, 61*(2), 647–672.

Lawrence, J. F., Capotosto, L., Branum-Martin, L., White, C., & Snow, C. (2012). Language proficiency, home-language status, and English vocabulary development: A longitudinal follow-up of the Word Generation program. *Bilingualism: Language and Cognition, 15*(3), 437–451.

Lawrence, J. F., White, C., & Snow, C. E. (2010). The words students need. *Educational Leadership*, 68(2), 22–26.

Lee, S. H., & Muncie. J. (2006). From receptive to productive: Improving ESL learners' use of vocabulary in a postreading composition task. *TESOL Quarterly*, 40(2). 295–320.

Lesaux, N. K., Kieffer, M. J., Kelley, J. G., & Harris, J. R. (2014). Effects of academic vocabulary instruction for linguistically diverse adolescents: Evidence from a randomized field trial. *American Educational Research Journal*, 51(6), 1159–1194.

Lesaux, N. K., & Kieffer, M. (2008). The role of derivational morphology in the reading comprehension of Spanish-speaking English language learners. *Reading and Writing*, 21(8), 783–804.

Lightbown, P. M. (2008). Transfer appropriate processing as a model for classroom second language acquisition. In Z. Han (Ed.), *Understanding Second Language Process*. Clevedon, UK: Multilingual Matters.

Lightbown, P. M., & Libben, G. (1984). The recognition and use of cognates by L2 learners. In R.W. Andersen (Ed.), *Second languages: A cross-linguistic perspective* (pp. 393–417). Rowley MA: Newbury House.

Lightbown., P. M., & Spada, N. (2013). *How languages are learned*, 4th Ed. Oxford: Oxford University Press.

MacSwan, J., Thompson, M. S., Rolstad, K., McAlister, K., & Lobo, G. (2017). Three theories of the effects of language education programs: An empirical evaluation of bilingual and English-only policies. *Annual Review of Applied Linguistics*, 37, 218–240.

Mancilla-Martinez, J., & Lesaux, N. K. (2011). Early home language use and later vocabulary development. *Journal of Educational Psychology*, 103, 535–546.

Martini, J. O. P. (2012). *High frequency vocabulary in a secondary Quebec ESL textbook corpus* (Unpublished master's thesis). Concordia University, Montreal, Canada.

Marzano, R. J. (2002). *Identifying the primary instructional concepts in mathematics: A linguistic approach*. Englewood, CO: Marzano and Associates.

Marzano, R. J. (2004). *Building background knowledge for academic achievement: Research on what works in schools*. Alexandria, VA: Association for Supervision and Curriculum Development.

Marzano, R. J., Kendall, J. S., & Paynter, D. E. (2005). A list of essential words by grade level. In S. Paynter, E. Bodrova, & J. Doty (Eds.), *For the love of words: Vocabulary instruction that works* (pp. 127–202). San Francisco: Jossey-Bass.

Matsuoka, W., & Hirsh, D. (2010). Vocabulary learning through reading: Does an ELT course book provide good opportunities? *Reading in a Foreign Language*, 22(1), 56–70.

Meara, P. M. (1980). Vocabulary acquisition: A neglected aspect of language learning. *Language Teaching and Linguistics Abstracts*, 13, 221–246.

Meara, P. M., & Miralpeix, I. (2016). *Tools for researching vocabulary*. Bristol: Multilingual Matters.

Milton, J. (2009). *Measuring second language vocabulary acquisition*. Bristol: Multilingual Matters.

Milton, J., & Meara, P. (1995). How periods abroad affect vocabulary growth in a foreign language. *ITL Review of Applied Linguistics*, 107–108, 17–34.

Moss, G. (1991). Cognate recognition: Its importance in teaching ESP reading courses to Spanish speakers. *English for Specific Purposes, 11*, 141–158.

Nagy, W. (2005). Why instruction needs to be long-term and comprehensive. In E. H. Hiebert & M. L. Kamil (Eds.), *Teaching and learning vocabulary* (pp. 27–44). Mahwah, NJ: Lawrence Erlbaum Associates.

Nagy, W. E., Garcia, G. E., Durgunoğlu, A. Y., & Hancin-Bhatt, B. (1993). Spanish–English bilingual students' use of cognates in English reading. *Journal of Reading Behavior, 25*, 241–259.

Nagy, W. E., Herman, P. A., & Anderson, R. C. (1985). Learning words from context. *Reading Research Quarterly, 20*(2), 233–253.

Nakata, T. (2008). English vocabulary learning with word lists, word cards and computers: Implications from cognitive psychology research for optimal spaced learning. *ReCALL, 20*(1), 3–20.

NALDIC. (no date). EAL pupils in schools: The latest statistics about EAL learners in our schools. Retrieved from: https://www.naldic.org.uk/research-and-information/eal-statistics/eal-pupils/

Nassaji, H. (2003). L2 vocabulary learning from context: Strategies, knowledge sources, and their relationship with success in L2 lexical inferencing. *TESOL Quarterly, 37*, 645–670.

Nation, I. S. P. (1990). *Teaching and learning vocabulary*. Boston: Heinle & Heinle.

Nation, I. S. P. (2001). *Learning vocabulary in another language*. Cambridge: Cambridge University Press.

Nation, I. S. P. (2006). How large a vocabulary is needed for reading and listening? *Canadian Modern Language Review, 63*(1), 59–82.

Nation, I. S. P. (2008). *Teaching vocabulary: Strategies and techniques*. Boston: Heinle.

Nation, I. S. P. (2012). *The BNC/COCA word family lists*. Retrieved from http://www.victoria.ac.nz/lals/about/staff/publications/paul-nation/Information-on-the-BNC_COCA-word-family-lists.pdf.

Nation, I. S. P. (2013). *Learning vocabulary in another language* (2nd ed.). Cambridge: Cambridge University Press.

Nation, I. S. P. (2018). Reading a whole book to learn vocabulary. *ITL (International Journal of Applied Linguistics), 169*(1), 30–43.

Nation, I. S. P. (no date). A brief critique of Hart, B. & Risley, T. (1995). Meaningful differences in the everyday experience of young American children https://www.victoria.ac.nz/lals/about/staff/publications/paul nation/HartandRisleycritique.pdf

Nation, I. S. P., & Beglar, D. (2007). A vocabulary size test. *The Language Teacher, 31*(7), 9–13.

Navés, T., Miralpeix, I., & Celaya, M. L. (2005). Who transfers more ... and what? Cross-linguistic influence in relation to school grade and language dominance in EFL. *International Journal of Multilingualism, 2*, 113–134.

NCES. (2015). Public high school 4-year adjusted cohort graduation rate (ACGR), by selected student characteristics and state: 2010-11 through 2013–14. In Digest of educational statistics. Retrieved from: https://nces.ed.gov/programs/digest/d15/tables/dt15_219.46.asp?refer=dropout

NCES. (2018). English language learners in public schools. In *The condition of education*. Retrieved from: https://nces.ed.gov/programs/coe/pdf/coe_cgf.pdf

Neuman, S. B., & Koskinen, P. S. (1992). Captioned television as comprehensible input: effects of incidental word learning from context for language minority students. *Reading Research Quarterly, 27*(1), 95–106.

O'Keeffe, A., McCarthy, M., & Carter, R. (2007). *From corpus to classroom: Language use and language teaching*. Cambridge: Cambridge University Press.

Otwinowska, A. (2016). Cognate vocabulary in language acquisition and use: Attitudes, awareness, activation. Bristol: Multilingual Matters.

Pacheco, M. B., & Goodwin, A. P. (2013). Putting two and two together: Middle school students' morphological problem-solving strategies for unknown words. *Journal of Adolescent & Adult Literacy, 56*(7), 541–553.

Paradis, J. (2007). Second language acquisition in childhood. In E. Hoff & M. Shatz, (Eds.), *Blackwell Handbook of Language Development*, Oxford: Blackwell Publishing Ltd. doi: 10.1002/9780470757833.ch19

Paribakht, T. S., & Wesche, M. (1996). Enhancing vocabulary acquisition through reading: A hierarchy of text-related exercise types. *The Canadian Modern Language Review, 52*(2), 155–178.

Paribakht, T. S., & Wesche, M. (1997). Vocabulary enhancement activities and reading for meaning in a second language. In J. Coady & T. Huckin (Eds.), *Second language vocabulary acquisition: A rationale for pedagogy* (pp. 174–200). New York: Cambridge University Press.

Pawley, A., & Syder, F. (1983). Two puzzles for linguistic theory; Nativelike selection and nativelike fluency. In J. C. Richards & R. Schmidt (Eds.), *Language and communication*. London: Longman.

Peters, E., & Webb, S. (2018). Incidental vocabulary acquisition through viewing L2 television and factors that affect learning. *Studies in Second Language Acquisition*. 1–27. 10.1017/S0272263117000407.

Pigada, M., & Schmitt, N. (2006). Vocabulary acquisition from extensive reading: A case study. *Reading in a Foreign Language, 18*(1), 1–28.

Poulisse, N., & Bongaerts, T. (1994). First language use in second language production. *Applied Linguistics, 15*(1), 36–57.

Que, C., & Horst, M. (2010, November). *Sushi bar and world culture: ESL learners' use of compound nouns*. Paper presented at the annual conference of La société pour la promotion de l'anglais, langue seconde, au Québec (SPEAQ), Quebec City.

Ramírez, G., Chen, X., Geva, E., & Luo, Y. (2011). Morphological awareness and word reading in English language learners: Evidence from Spanish- and Chinese-speaking children. *Applied Psycholinguistics, 32*, 601–618. doi:10.1017/S0142716411000233

Reppen, R. (2010). *Using corpora in the language classroom*. Cambridge: Cambridge University Press.

Reynolds, D. W. (2005). Linguistic correlates of second language literacy development: Evidence from middle-grade learner essays. *Journal of Second Language Writing, 14*, 19–45.

Roberts, T. A. (2009). *No limits to literacy for preschool English learners*. Thousand Oaks, CA: Corwin.

Rodgers, M. P. H., & Webb, S. (2011). Narrow viewing: the vocabulary in related television programs. *TESOL Quarterly, 45*(4), 689–717.

Saffran, J., Aslin, R., & Newport, E. (1996). Statistical learning by 8-month-old infants. *Science, 274,* 1926.

Saville-Troike, M. (1984). What really matters in second language learning for academic achievement? *TESOL Quarterly, 18,* 199–219.

Schmidt, R. (2001). Attention. In P. Robinson (Ed.), *Cognition and second language instruction* (pp. 3–32). Cambridge: Cambridge University Press.

Schmitt, N. (2000). History of vocabulary in language learning. In *Vocabulary in language teaching.* Cambridge: Cambridge University Press.

Schmitt, N. (2008). Review article: Instructed second language vocabulary learning. *Language Teaching Research, 12,* 329–363.

Schmitt, N., Jiang, X., & Grabe, W. (2011). The percentage of words known in a text and reading comprehension. *Modern Language Journal, 95*(1), 26–43.

Schmitt, N., & Schmitt, D. (2014). A reassessment of frequency and vocabulary size in L2 vocabulary teaching. *Language Teaching, 47,* 484–503.

Schmitt, N., Schmitt, D., & Clapham, C. (2001). Developing and exploring the behaviour of two new versions of the Vocabulary Levels Test. Language, *Testing, 18*(1), 55–88.

Schmitt, N., & Zimmerman, C. B. (2002). Derivative word forms: What do learners know? *TESOL Quarterly, 36*(2), 145–171.

Scott, J. A., Miller, T. F., & Flinsbach, S. L. (2012). Developing word consciousness: Lessons from highly diverse fourth-grade classrooms. In E. J. Kame'enui & J. J. Baumann (Eds.), *Vocabulary instruction: Research to practice* (2nd ed.) (pp. 169–188). New York, NY: Guilford Press.

Scott, J., Nagy, B., & Flinsbach, S. (2008). More than merely words: Redefining vocabulary learning in a culturally and linguistically diverse society. In A. Farstrup & J. Samuels (Eds.), *What research has to say about vocabulary instruction* (pp. 182–210). Newark, DE: International Reading Association.

Scott, J. A., Skobell, B. J., & Wells, J. (2016). *The word-conscious classroom: Building the vocabulary readers and writers need.* Santa Cruz, CA: Text Project Inc.

Segalowitz, N. (2010). *Cognitive bases of second language fluency.* New York: Routledge.

Short, D. J., & Fitzsimmons, S. (2007). *Double the work: Challenges and solutions to acquiring language and academic literacy for adolescent English language learners. Report to Carnegie Corporation of New York.* New York: Alliance for Excellent Education.

Skinner, B. F. (1957). *Verbal behavior.* New York: Appleton-Century-Crofts.

Spada, N., & Lightbown, P. M. (2008). Form-focused instruction: Isolated or Integrated? *TESOL Quarterly, 42,* 181–207.

Snow, C. E., & Hoefnagel-Höhle, M. (1978). The critical period for language acquisition: Evidence from second language learning. *Child Development, 49*(4), 1114–1128.

Springer, S., & Collins, L. (2008). Interacting inside and outside of the language classroom. *Language Teaching Research, 12*(1), 39-60.

Stæhr, L. S. (2008). Vocabulary size and the skills of listening, reading and writing. *Language Learning Journal, 36,* 139–152.

Stanovich, K. E. (1986). Matthew effects in reading: Some consequences of individual differences in the acquisition of literacy. *Reading Research Quarterly, 21,* 360–407.

Stemach, G., & Williams, W. (1988). *WordExpress: The first 2,500 words of spoken English.* Novato, CA: Academic Therapy Publications.

Swain, M. (1985). Communicative competence: Some roles of comprehensible input and comprehensible output in its development. In S. Gass & C. Madden (Eds.), *Input in second language acquisition* (pp. 235–253). Rowley, MA: Newbury House.

Swanborn, M. S. L., & de Glopper, K. (1999). Incidental word learning while reading: A meta-analysis. *Review of Educational Research, 69*(3), 261–285.

Sylvén, L. K., & Sundqvist, P. (2012). Gaming as extramural English L2 learning and L2 proficiency among young learners. *ReCALL, 24,* 302–321.

Tomasello, M. (2003). *Constructing a language: A usage-based theory of language acquisition.* Cambridge, MA: Harvard University Press.

Uchikoshi, Y. (2006). English vocabulary development in bilingual kindergarteners: What are the best predictors? *Bilingualism: Language and Cognition, 9,* 33–49.

Uchikoshi, Y. (2014). Development of vocabulary in Spanish-speaking and Cantonese-speaking English Language Learners. *Applied Psycholinguistics, 35*(1), 119–153.

Umbel, V. M., Pearson, B. Z., Fernàndez, M. C., & Oller, D. K. (1992). Measuring bilingual children's receptive vocabularies. *Child Development, 63,* 1012–1020.

Ur, P. (1981). *Discussions that work: Task-centered fluency practice.* Cambridge: Cambridge University Press.

Van Ek, J. A., & Trim, J. L. M. (1990). *Threshold 1990.* Strasbourg: Council of Europe Publishing.

Van Ek, J. A., & Trim, J. L. M. (1991). *Waystage 1990.* Strasbourg: Council of Europe Publishing.

Van Zeeland, H. (2014). Lexical inferencing in first and second language listening. *Modern Language Journal, 98*(4), 1006-1021.

Van Zeeland, H., & Schmitt, N. (2013). Lexical coverage in L1 and L2 listening comprehension: The same or different from reading comprehension? *Applied Linguistics, 34*(4), 457–479.

Verhallen, M., & Schoonen, R. (1993). Lexical knowledge of monolingual and bilingual children. *Applied Linguistics, 14,* 344–363.

Vermeer, A. (2001). Breadth and depth of vocabulary in relation to L1/L2 acquisition and frequency of input. *Applied Psycholinguistics, 22,* 217–234.

Vygotsky, L. (1978). *Mind in society.* Cambridge, MA: Harvard University Press.

Wang, J. (no date). How to read Chinese compound words by understanding root characters. Retrieved from https://www.yoyochinese.com/blog/how-to-read-chinese-compound-words-understanding-root-characters.

Waring, R. (1997). A study of receptive and productive learning from word cards. *Studies in Foreign Languages and Literature, 21,* 94–114.

Webb, S. (2007). The effects of repetition on vocabulary knowledge. *Applied Linguistics, 28*(1), 46–65.

Webb, S., & Chang, A. C.-S. (2012). Second language vocabulary growth. *RELC Journal, 43*(1), 113–26.

Webb, S., & Nation, P. (2017). *How vocabulary is learned.* Oxford: Oxford University Press.

Webb, S., & Rodgers, M. P. H. (2009). The lexical coverage of movies. *Applied Linguistics, 30*(3), 407–427.

Webb, S., Sasao, Y., & Ballance, O. (2017). The updated Vocabulary Levels Test: Developing and validating two new forms of the VLT. *ITL - International Journal of Applied Linguistics, 168*(1), 34–70.

West, M. (1953). *A general service list of English words*. London: Longman.

White, J., & Horst, M. (2012). Cognate awareness-raising in late childhood: Teachable and useful. *Language Awareness, 21*, 181–196.

Winitz, H., Gillespie, B., & Starcev, J. (1995). The development of English speech patterns of a 7-year-old Polish-speaking child. *Journal of Psycholinguistic Research, 24*, 117–143.

Zahar, R., Cobb, T. & Spada, N. (2001). Acquiring vocabulary through reading: Effects of frequency and contextual richness. *Canadian Modern Language Review, 15*(4), 541–572.

Zeno, S. M., Ivens, S. H., Millard, R. T., & Duvvuri, R. (1995). *The educator's word frequency guide*. Brewster, NY: Touchstone Applied Science Associates, Inc.

Zimmerman, C. B. (1997). Historical trends in second language vocabulary instruction. In J. Coady & T. Huckin (Eds.), *Second language vocabulary acquisition: A rationale for pedagogy* (pp. 5–19). New York: Cambridge University Press.

Zipf, G. K. (1935). *The psychology of language*. Houghton-Mifflin.

Zipf, G. K. (1949). *Human behavior and the principle of least effort*. Addison-Wesley.

Index

Page numbers annotated with 'g' refer to glossary entries.

academic vocabulary 13–15, 18–24, 55–67, 91–100, 102–11, 113–21, 133–4, 149g
Academic Word List (AWL) 19–21, 23, 56–7, 94, 108–9, 113, 119–20, 149g
adolescent learners of English 101–29
   academic vocabulary 102–11, 113–21
   learning strategies 112–14, 121–30
affixed words 32–3, 98–9, 121, 135–6, 139, 149g
age, effect on language learning 80, 111–14, 124–5, 138
alphabetic systems 31–2, 149g
Arabic-speaking learners of English 31
automaticity 28, 33, 134, 149g

basic interpersonal communicative skills (BICS) 56, 92, 149g
behaviorism 39–41, 149g
bilingualism 38–9, 77–9, 112–14, 115–18
British National Corpus (BNC) 10–11, 22–3

Catalan-speaking learners of English 117–18
Chinese-speaking learners of English 31, 81–3, 101
chunks 34–5, 136, 150g
classroom interaction 5–7, 24–5, 44–6, 64–6, 115–16, 125–6, 131–2, 134–5
cognates 33, 63, 84–7, 96, 117, 121, 138, 150g
   cognate awareness 84–6, 121, 150g
cognitive academic language proficiency (CALP) 56–8, 74–5, 93, 111–13, 150g
collocations 27, 34–5, 134, 150g
communicative competence 70, 150g
communicative skills 56, 92, 149g
compound words 81–3, 150g
comprehensible input 60–3, 150g
computer games 64
concordances 50–2, 126–9, 150g
connectionist theory 41–2, 150g
Content and Language Integrated Learning (CLIL) 75
contextual guessing 63, 99–100, 122–6, 139

Corpus of Contemporary American English (COCA) 10–12, 22–3
corpus/corpora 10–12, 22–3, 126–9, 151g
coverage 11–15, 60–2, 122, 132, 137, 151g
Danish-speaking learners of English 106–8, 124–5
declarative knowledge 47–8, 151g
decoding 18–19, 32, 80, 133–4, 151g
derivation 10, 82–3, 98–9, 114–16, 121–2, 126, 135–6, 151g
dictionaries 12
discourse 16–17, 151g
domain-specific vocabulary 16, 21–2, 92, 132, 151g
Dutch-speaking learners of English 115
elaborative processing 46, 50–4, 63, 96–7, 136, 151g
   concordancing 125–7
   keyword mnemonics 53–4, 153g
   word maps 34, 96
English language learners (ELLs) 16, 18–19
   foreign language contexts 106–8
   immersion contexts 77–9
   minority-language students 76, 108–9, 113–14
English-speaking learners of Dutch 111
expository texts 19, 55–8, 92, 120, 147, 151g
eye-tracking studies 63
'false friends' 86, 117, 139
families 43–4, 57, 75–7, 111
film viewing 63–4
first language (L1) 8, 19, 152g
   influence on L2 learning 80–7, 133
   vocabulary size 106, 108–9, 132
foreign language contexts 106–8
form 29–32, 135
formulaic sequences 34–5, 136, 152g
French-speaking learners of English 25, 85–6, 88–90, 116–7
frequency-based tests 103–8

games 64
genres 152g
graded readers 16, 39, 114, 119, 152g
grammatical function 35
headwords 10, 152g
high school students *see* adolescent learners of English
high-frequency words 16–17, 92, 109–11, 119, 131–2, 136–37
home environment 43–4, 57, 75–7, 111
incidental learning hypothesis 59–60, 152g
incidental vocabulary learning 58–66, 108–10, 137–8, 152g
independent learning 60–4, 66, 98, 100, 113–14, 121–30
inequality 43–4, 111, 118–21
inferencing skills 121–6 *see also* learning strategies
inflection 11, 32–3, 152g *see also* morphological awareness
information books (expository texts) 19, 55–8, 92, 120, 147, 151g
information-processing models 44–8, 56–8, 66, 153g
informed judgment 92–3
integrated form-focused instruction 44–6, 153g
intentional vocabulary learning 59, 62, 73–5, 91–100, 109–11, 113–14, 118–21, 134–6, 138–9, 153g
interdependence hypothesis 38, 153g

Japanese-speaking learners of English 31, 70, 129–30
keyword mnemonics 53–4, 153g
knowledge 5–36
  partial-precise continuum 24–6
  receptive-productive continuum 27–30, 47–8, 88–90, 134–6, 151g, 155g
  vocabulary depth 26–7, 90–1, 96–100
known-word coverage 11–15, 60–2, 122, 132, 137, 151g

learner corpus/corpora 153g *see also* corpus/corpora
learning environments
  foreign language contexts 106–8
  immersion contexts 77–9
learning goals 10–21, 131
learning strategies 63, 66, 81–7, 96–100, 112–14, 121–30, 138–9
  concordancing activities 126–9
  contextual guessing 99–100, 122–6, 139
  developing cognate awareness 84–85, 122, 150g

developing morphological awareness 80, 83–4, 87, 115, 122, 154g
inferencing skills 121–7
keyword mnemonics 53–4, 153g
word cards 40–1, 49–50, 128–30, 138
lemmas 10, 153g
lexical ability 113–114
lexical frequency profiling tools 12, 17, 54–5, 95, 120, 137, 153g
lexical richness 88–90, 116–18, 154g
lexicon, definition 154g
loanwords 33, 154g
low-frequency words 17–18, 92, 132, 136, 154g

Mandarin Chinese *see* Chinese-speaking learners of English
memory (phonological memory) 80, 155g
metalinguistic awareness 79–80, 87, 112–13, 115–16, 138, 154g
Middle School Vocabulary Lists (MSVL) 20–3, 56–7, 93–6, 118–9, 154g
mid-frequency words 11, 17, 93, 108–9, 110–11, 119, 154g
minority languages 76, 108–9
mnemonics 53–4, 153g
morphological awareness 32–3, 80, 83, 98–9, 115, 121–2, 126, 154g
morphology 32–3, 154g
motivation 44–6, 62
multi-word units 34–5, 154g

noticing 44, 48–9, 63, 125, 155g
orthography (writing) 116–18, 155g
  alphabetic systems 31–2, 149g

parent-child interaction 42–4, 57, 75–7, 111
partial-precise knowledge 24–6
Peabody Picture Vocabulary Test (PPVT) 71, 72–3, 111
phonological awareness 31–2, 79–80, 135, 155g
phonological memory 80, 155g
Picture Vocabulary Size Test (PVST) 71–2, 103
polysemy 33–4, 90–1, 136, 155g
pragmatics 33, 155g
preschool children 42–4, 57, 111, 137
primary school children *see* young learners of English
procedural knowledge 48, 155g
productive knowledge 27–30, 155g
proficiency 12, 38, 70, 102, 107, 109–19, 125, 133
Putonghua (Mandarin Chinese) *see* Chinese-speaking learners of English

reading 13–15, 16, 28, 46–7, 55–67, 132
  effect of socioeconomic status on 43–4, 57, 111, 119–21
  expository texts 19, 22, 55–8, 92, 120, 147
  graded readers 16, 109, 113, 152g
  incidental vocabulary learning 58–66, 109–10, 112–13
  reading aloud 57, 65–7
  sight words 55
  stories 57, 91–2, 133–4
  textbooks 13, 94, 109–10
receptive knowledge 27–30, 155g
register 35, 155g
retelling activities 50, 63
retrieval 40–1, 48–50, 156g
rich instruction 52, 96–100, 119–21, 136, 156g
second language (L2) 8, 156g
secondary school children *see* adolescent learners of English
semantics 33–4, 156g
sequential bilinguals 38, 112–14, 115–18, 156g
sight words 55, 156g
simultaneous bilinguals 38–9, 156g
sociocultural theory 63–6
socioeconomic status (SES) 44–5, 57, 75–7, 118–21, 156g
Spanish-speaking learners of English 24–6, 38–9, 46–7, 75–84, 101–2, 111–12, 115–18
stories 57, 91–2, 133–4
teaching methods 8–10, 118–29
  bilingual education programs 77–9
  concordancing activities 125–7
  Content and Language Integrated Learning (CLIL) 75
  rich instruction 52, 96–100, 119–21, 136
  selection of words 91–6, 118–21, 131–2
  word cards 40–1, 49–50, 128–9, 137–38
television viewing 63–4
Test de Vocabulario en Imagenes Peabody (TVIP) 72
tests
  frequency-based tests 71–2, 103–9
  Peabody Picture Vocabulary Test (PPVT/TVIP) 71–3, 108
  Picture Vocabulary Size Test (PVST) 71–2, 103
  Vocabulary Knowledge Scale (VKS) 25–6
  Vocabulary Levels Test (VLT) 104, 106–8
  Vocabulary Size Test (VST) 71–2, 103–5
textbooks 13, 94, 109–10
theories 37–67
  behaviorism 40–2
  comprehensible input 60–3

connectionist theory 41–2
information-processing models 44–8, 56–8, 66
interdependence hypothesis 38, 133
sociocultural theory 63–65
usage-based theory 41–4
transfer-appropriate processing hypothesis (TAP) 47, 156g
Turkish-speaking learners of Dutch 91
type of processing-resource allocation hypothesis (TOPRA) 46–7, 156g
usage-based theory 41–4, 156g
VocabProfile (software tool) 11, 17, 54–5, 95, 119, 137
vocabulary depth 26–7, 90–1, 96–100, 157g
Vocabulary Knowledge Scale (VKS) 25–6
vocabulary size 12–15, 33, 54–5, 137, 157g
  adolescents 102–11
  young children 69–77, 79–87, 91
Vocabulary Levels Test (VLT) 104, 106–8
Vocabulary Size Test (VST) 71–2, 103–5
word cards 40–1, 49–50, 128–29, 137–8
word families 10–21, 103–11, 132, 157g
Word Generation 120–1
word maps 34, 96, 157g
word-part knowledge (morphological awareness) 32–3, 79, 83, 98–9, 115, 121–2, 126, 154g
writing 115–117, 155g
  alphabetic systems 31–32, 149g
young learners of English 69–100, 133–4
  influence of first language 79, 81–7, 133
  preschool children 42–4, 57
  vocabulary depth 90–1, 96–100
  vocabulary size 69–77, 79–87, 91
Zipf's law 61–2, 157g

www.ingramcontent.com/pod-product-compliance
Ingram Content Group UK Ltd.
Pitfield, Milton Keynes, MK11 3LW, UK
UKHW022231230426
12048UKWH00016BA/1193